Help Them Help YOU
Manage-Lead

Help Them Help YOU

Manage-Lead

Using 9 Educating Approaches
to Encourage Engagement,
Retention, Performance Improvement,
and Personal Development

Stephen W. Hobbs, Ed.D.

Help Them Help You Manage-Lead

E-Book ISBN: 978-0-9783966-5-7
Paperback ISBN: 978-0-9783966-4-0

Additional copies of this book may be ordered by visiting the
PPG Online Bookstore at:

shop.polishedpublishinggroup.com

Due to the dynamic nature of the Internet, any website addresses mentioned within this book may have been changed or discontinued since publication.

Legal Notice

The Publisher has strived to be as accurate and complete as possible in the creation of this book, notwithstanding the fact that The Publisher does not warrant or represent at any time that the contents within are accurate due to the rapidly changing nature of management and leadership within organizations.

While all attempts have been made to verify information provided in this publication, The Publisher assumes no responsibility for errors, omissions, or contrary interpretation of the subject matter herein. Any perceived slights of specific persons, peoples, or organizations are unintentional.

Readers are cautioned to rely on their own judgment about their individual circumstances to act according to the insights provided herein.

Please refrain from distributing this work in any format to others without the explicit written consent of the author.

Published by
WELLth Learning Network Inc.

For information, address correspondence to:

WELLth Learning Network
Box 63043 Stadium RPO
Calgary, Alberta, Canada
T2N 4S5

info@managingleading.com
info@wellthlearning.com
1.403.875.0449

Testimonials

If managing as a leader is your game, this book is a must read. Just like all great leaders, Stephen Hobbs doesn't tell you what to do or not to do. Instead, he models exquisite leadership skills through this comprehensive guidebook that should be required reading. Using fabulous metaphors and real life leadership problems to overcome, Stephen expertly leads the way to a new realm of leadership possibility.

Shawne Duperon
Six-time EMMY® winner, ShawneTV

As a fellow colleague and avid admirer of "Hobbit's" work, I highly recommend this book for consultants and facilitators in the Organizational Development space as a crucial "handbook" of new thought, new approaches and best practices. Step into Stephen's mind, for even a second, and see the world of infinite possibilities, as he "plays with words, thoughts, practices and provocative stories" to challenge traditional approaches and methods we use with clients. It is wonderful to finally see all the stories and examples he uses when we've co-educated finally transposed onto paper. This book is as large as Steven's heart and only a morsel of what he has yet to write and share with the world!

Laurie Maslak, Ph.D.
Principal Consultant with Maslak & Associates Inc.

It's true! Manager-leaders are positioned to situationally educate their staff. It was true for me when I managed and led in an oil and gas company, and a government agency. I experienced how my influence grew as I properly educated myself and my staff. Dr Stephen Hobbs' book hits the mark! His simple and concise approach of the 9 educating approaches, whatever the type or size organization, provide a catalyst to help new manager-leaders grow their influence. It will help established manager-leaders to improve their practice and leap-frog them ahead in engaging their staff, improving performance, support succession planning and further personal development. This is simply a MUST BUY book!

Teresa de Grosbois
 3X Bestselling author
Chair Evolutionary Business Council

In his latest book, *Help Them Help YOU to Manage-Lead*, Stephen Hobbs has done a masterful job in summarizing his 40 years of experience as a leading edge educator into nine practical educational approaches that will help managers lead and leaders manage more effectively. A must read for aspiring managers and leaders who are looking for tools that, if applied, would help them go from good to to better than great!

Richard & Lillas Marie Hatala
Co-authors of *Integrative Leadership: Building a Foundation for Personal, Professional and Organizational Success*
Co-Founders of 'Integrative Leadership International Ltd.

Steve,

Thanks for giving me the opportunity to read your book on discovering the *9 educating approaches* helpful for managing and leading others.

I enjoyed reading the book (actually twice to get the full essence) and wish it had been available earlier in my career. I would have been much more effective in my educating approach.

The wonderful thing about the reading experience was that I knew the methods in general through other learning I have had, but it was never presented in a concise and organized manner as presented in this book.

I also found the terminology that you used in Chapters 5 to 7 to describe the nine approaches to be a lot more correlated to the concepts presented and, because of that, easier to remember when I encounter a situational leading/managing challenge.

The distinction between commitment and estimate presented in Chapter 8 actually took me by surprise. I now know why in the past I was disappointed in my ability to get some of the team members to deliver on the 'promises' they made. Obviously, they were giving me their 'promise of an estimate' which I mistook for 'commitment'. Well things are going to be different going forward – there will no doubt be clarity in expectations. The 7 major commitments cited in Chapter 8 will no doubt provide an excellent reminder to me on a daily basis. (I plan to put it them up on my desktop opening page until they are ingrained in my mind.)

As I mentioned to you in our conversation, I am in the phase of my career where I need to generate continuity of knowledge that would be essential to the emerging young leaders in my organization. This knowledge is gained from experience in the subject matter field such as regulatory reforms in transportation industry. There are no textbooks around that can be accessed by the young leaders to educate themselves. So at least for me, this book has arrived just in time. Connecting the leading and managing with the 9 approaches to educating is going to be a very productive process.

I learned about action mapping the first time at the leadership course you taught. Chapter 11 solidified the concepts for me, particularly the 9+1 suggestions regarding starting with Self.

Steve, this book is exciting and well written. I am certain it will be a hit with the new generations of leaders.

Let me finish by sharing a quick note for those sales letters you will write:

Steve Hobbs' presentation of the *9 educating approaches* helpful for leading and managing stimulates the mind and will evoke a level of confidence in the minds of young, emergent leaders. It's a win-win approach for both the educators and their learners!

Dr. Deepak Ekbote
B.Sc., M.Sc. Ph.D. M.B.A.
Canadian Transportation Company

If you have staff, employees, volunteers, family, friends, colleagues, clients, or customers whom you manage and lead, it is critical that you know how to use nine interrelated educating approaches when you manage and lead.

People are constantly learning!

When you help others to achieve their dreams, you help them take huge strides in living their great lives.

Similarly, you live your great life through educating what you enjoy learning. In this give and take exchange, everyone flourishes and grows.

Take it a step further with your customers and clients. When you manage and lead your relationships, then learning and educating are the cornerstones of your collective accomplishments. When YOU find ways for your customers and clients to say "I need your help", you are on the path to great working relationships for years to come.

You are constantly educating!

As you manage and lead all of your relationships, let the 9 educating approaches outlined in this book serve you in (learning) how to Help Them Help YOU Manage-Lead.

Foreword

Educating ourselves and those we lead is essential for remaining relevant in our ever changing world. I witnessed this first-hand while spending a year interviewing leaders and managers of highly-successful businesses. Those who weathered the storms of economic uncertainty and thrived had an unwavering commitment to life-long learning. Attracting and retaining quality talent doesn't happen by accident, but by design. Maintaining strong bonds with those you serve depends on it, as what happens on the inside of a company eventually shows up on the outside.

In Help Them Help YOU Manage-Lead, Stephen Hobbs zeros in on nine approaches to engage, retain, develop people, and improve their performance, while drawing out a genuine sense of fulfillment. Leaders are learners, which is probably what inspired you to pick up this book. In reading, you'll discover that Stephen offers more than quality content. He designed the book to bring YOU into it, making it your own personal guide to powerfully knowing which educating approach to use in any given situation.

I'll keep this book on hand and reference it often, as I'm sure you will too. It will expand your awareness, ability to listen, discern, and respond consciously in a way that activates the potential within and grows inspired future leaders.

Marilyn Suttle, bestselling author of *Who's Your Gladys: How to Turn Even the Most Difficult Customer Into Your Biggest Fan*

Acknowledgements

To those who educate,
To those who learn, and
To those willing
to improve both
for the benefit
of themselves
and those with
whom they share
their stories!

Table of Contents

Preface

This book highlights the conceptual and practical linkages among managing, leading and the *9 Educating Approaches*. These linkages help YOU manage-lead others, no matter the type and size of your organization anywhere in the world.

This book is premised on the saying:

When you listen, you learn;
when you share, you educate

Therefore, everyone learns as everyone educates.

When you manage and lead, it is helpful to know how people learn and how you educate. In this book, the emphasis is on *9 educating approaches* useful to fulfill the mantra:

Help Them Help YOU Manage-Lead

From There to Here

The term 'knowledge worker,' borne from the Industrial Age into the Digital Age, describes and explains many people in many organizations.

For every knowledge worker, learning is a common denominator. Therefore, learning is a baseline connector that must be nurtured for organizations and employees to be the best for the world.

Nurturing employee relationships within the organization is a recurring issue faced by manager-leaders. With the constant pressure to do more in support of employees, manager-leaders are seeking insights from others. Traditionally, they turn to management and leadership knowledge captured within organizational best practices initiatives. They are often obtained through the company Intranet, Internet searches, reading books, and/or from coaches and mentors.

It's interesting to note that even with all of this information available, the connection between management and leadership theory and practice seems to be lagging. Putting 'knowing into doing' is a gap that needs more awareness. In other words, what is needed is a way for you to enact managing and leading that inspires and motivates others to action.

This book presents such a 'way'. It suggests you can use 9 educating approaches to Help Them Help YOU to Manage-Lead.

In an effort to personalize this book
that is, to have you read this book
as though it was written for YOU
I use the term 'you' instead
of generic terms like
manager and leader.

Also, the beauty in using 'you', is that it can be plural as well as singular.
Therefore, I encourage you to read this book with three colleagues.
You will engage in meaningful dialogue about what you are learning about:

Help Them Help YOU Manage-Lead

Motivation and Inspiration

Motivating and inspiring others at work involves finding ways to help them learn and sustain their learning through effective and relevant application. In doing so, you significantly influence individual achievements and the accomplishments of groups. Through workplace educating you help 'get things done' in an efficient and successful manner, all the while sustaining the well-being of each person.

This real engagement is fostered through promoting, embracing, and integrating educating approaches into your work. Once you purposefully learn and apply the tools and techniques of workplace educating, you move with ease and grace among those you manage and lead.

Some of you use educating approaches consciously while others of you are new to their use.

Which one are you?

Whatever your response, this book will:
- Enhance what you already know and practice, and/or
- Provide insights, tips, and techniques to start your new journey

Content of the Book

The focus of this book is the connection among managing, leading, and workplace educating. It presents a way to engage the hands, heads, and hearts of others through the identification and demonstration of *9 educating approaches*.

Also, the book's message encourages you to describe and explain the educating approach(es) you are using to others, so they might value how it works in their performance improvement and personal development.

Because learning is a key process in organizational life, you can use these educating approaches as a way to foster and fashion learning that helps people live their great lives while creating the well-living workplace. This involvement, in turn, increases self-enablement and empowerment when shared with others.

The key message of this book is to use educating approaches in managing and leading. To do so increases the likelihood of engaging others. When people are engaged, they stay around longer. They improve their performance and thus increase productivity. Therefore, by reading this book you have everything to gain in your own personal development as well.

If *management and leadership* are terms and concepts that are not that well known to you, this book can help. However, other resources should also be consulted to continue your learning.

Chapters

The Book is divided into 12 Chapters.

Chapter 1 provides an **Introduction** to the topic of this book. The learning outcomes for the book are listed at the end of this Chapter.

Chapter 2 establishes a relationship between **Management and Leadership**. These two organizational tasks are complementary and inextricably linked—you cannot have one without the other. You cannot have a coin without two sides. You cannot have managing without leading and vice versa.

Chapter 3 connects **Educating with Managing and Leading.** This chapter makes the case for managers and leaders to use the *9 educating approaches* as ways to engage the hands, heads, and hearts of others. The visual model supporting subsequent chapters is introduced.

Chapter 4 ties **Work-Related Learning and Development with Educating** through outlining the meaning of the terms *learning, knowing,* and *educating*.

Chapter 5 introduces the trinity of educating approaches broadly called **Teacher**. The three approaches are instructing, training and consulting. These three approaches encourage you to **teach on the reach**; that is, they encourage you to **Reach Out** to involve others.

Chapter 6 introduces coaching, shifting and counselling. These three approaches are called **Guide**. They encourage you to be a **guide on the ride**; that is, they have you **Reaching With** others to get things done.

Chapter 7 is about the **Sage,** also referred to as the **sage off the page**. The Sage connects facilitating, mentoring, and minstrelling. Through these three approaches you encourage others in **Reaching From** the near future to value what is needed today.

Chapter 8 integrates the *9 educating approaches* under the banner of **Educator Within**. After reading this chapter, you will have more options to choose from when managing and leading.

Chapter 9 presents an explicit **connection between the *9 educating approaches***, and managing and leading. Woven into this chapter is the importance of making commitments. This topic is included to highlight the significance of your connection with the material presented in the book and your subsequent implementing of the approach(es) most suited to the situation.

Chapter 10 connects the dots between **engagement, retention, and performance improvement** when using the *9 educating approaches*. In addition, it reminds you how your competence in educating approaches contributes to your **management-leadership progress**. When choosing between two candidates, the one with proficiency in *educating approaches* has an advantage.

Chapter 11 involves making the learning real. It is one thing for you to learn something; it is yet another thing for you to do something with what you have learned. This identifies what comes next when you transfer your learning from this book to your workplace. The chapter involves **Taking IT to Work** through **Action Mapping.**

Chapter 12 offers closing remarks to encourage your continue involvement with the 9 educating approaches, and managing and leading.

In combination, these 11 chapters provide a rich starting point to **Help Them Help YOU Manage-Lead**. Discovering the linkages between managing and leading and the *9 educating approaches* adds to your versatility and resilience. That versatility and resilience will carry you forward in today's workplace.

Here is the overview model
through which this book will unfold.
Variations of this model will appear
throughout the book.

More in-depth explanations of this model begin in Chapter 3.

Let me introduce you to the Minstrel (see figure in the middle of the drawing.) This figure is a caricature I developed 35+ years ago as I began writing poetry and exploring what I have come to know as the mysteries of life. The figure has grown in stature and intensity. However, it continues to represent the connection with the whole. Also, the figure is drawn so that it faces away from you because the minstrel is YOU.

My Path

I am educating without
From an educator within

I ask for opportunities
That allow me to be
With others who care
To create something
Bigger than what we
Can do alone

I ask for learners
Who care enough
About themselves and others
That they will study
The great mysteries,
Then find ways to share
What they learn
So they might know
Themselves even more

I ask that my work
Be made known
To the one and the many,
And that my work
be expanded upon
And enthused
In the halls
And along the paths
Of the world every day

I seek to be alive
With learners as leaders,
Leaders as learners,
Leaders as educators,
Educators as leaders

I am who I am becoming
And I've become who I am
Through educating
Myself and others

With staff in hand,
Heart on my sleeve,
Head present,
Soul and spirit as my educators
I am educating without
From an educator within

August 24, 2005
SWHobbs

Chapter 1:
Introduction

****

Each day you find yourself in situations where managing and leading involves dealing with work-related learning and development. You're called upon to educate others in doing something in a better way, share new ideas, and/or guide people in their decision making.

Consider the following questions:

1. Are you consciously attuned and attentive to work situations in which you help others to help you manage and lead? And are you looking for more insights?

2. Are you confused about how best to deal with work-related learning and development situations, and yet you intuitively help others to help you manage and lead?

3. Are you struggling to figure out how to inspire and motivate others? And are you looking for new insights in how to do this?

4. Are you faced with potential staff engagement, retention, and/or performance improvement issues?

5. Are you considering a move up the corporate ladder and looking for a differentiator between you and other candidates?

If you answered 'yes' to any of these questions, this book will help.

Whether you're seasoned at managing and leading or emerging into this area, there are many pearls of wisdom within the pages of this book.

If you have been exposed to managing, leading, and educating (whether separately and/or together), then you already have experiences to draw from as you read this book. You are with some *knowing* now.

After reading the book, your *knowing* will increase. And when you apply your *knowing,* your knowledge and skill will increase.

Attending Workshops

In the past, perhaps you've read books and/or attended educator workshops focused on topics like 'Leader as Coach' or 'Manager as Facilitator', or perhaps combined workshops like 'Leader as Coach and Counsellor.' Many of these programs likely helped you improve how you go about your work.

Hopefully, you learnt that it's important to employ the correct educating approach to meet the unique needs of the specific situation. For example: If you have new staff join your department after working in similar jobs at another organization, it would be helpful to facilitate their engagement, and then train them for performance improvement, followed by coaching to retain their involvement.

When you misuse educating approaches, you may confuse yourself and those you interact with. When you use a particular educating approach, you have to ensure the name *identifier* matches the appropriate *action*.

> For example, when staff is looking for training from a manager who primarily coaches, it can be confusing and frustrating for everyone.
>
> Similarly, staff will get frustrated when looking for coaching and encouragement and they experience a leader who primarily trains.
>
> In other words, when your *actions* are not linked with the *terms and concepts* used to describe and explain the educating approach, it is likely others will become dissatisfied. This dissatisfaction then leads to lower productivity, increased costs, and, most importantly, compromised trust. People begin to think that you as a manager-leader are not 'walking your talk.'

On the surface, this mix-up of words may not seem like a big deal. However, over time, as the awareness of what works and what is needed within the workforce increases, you have to match what you *say* with what you *do*.

Action must accompany *intention of action*.

To prepare others to work along this managing and leading continuum, you have to help them learn how to help you manage and lead.

Key Concept

To encourage this shared journey, those who work with you must know how you are educating in order for them to share the management-leadership theory and managing-leading practice you are sharing with them. For your staff to value coaching as a way to improve their performance, they must comprehend what coaching is and how it works for performance improvement. When they value coaching and recognize its importance, then they can learn and use it with those they educate. The ripple effect becomes the norm!

Also, when you invite others into your workspace, you must be aware of their educating approaches. If required, you must help educate them in the *educating approach* needed for the situation. When others join you, they have experience in *educating approaches* aligned with particular work situations. Now they are in a new situation and adjustments are required. Sometimes those adjustments are subtle; sometimes they require considerable effort. Training and instructing in one organization can look different than it does in another organization.

It is important to ensure that new people have the correct terminology for the type of educating approach they'll use. Otherwise, they will confuse those they educate. It's better to (a) define the terms and concepts and (b) agree on the terms and concepts before applying the practices associated with the terms and concepts.

You must continually ask yourself, "What educating approach works best for this situation?" Make no assumptions! Keep reflecting on your practice. This book is a great outline of the 9 educating approaches from concept to suggested practices.

Active Involvement

When you are actively involved in the education process, others are more likely to be motivated and inspired. Through purposeful education, when individual and group accountabilities are made explicit, there is reduced duplicity and reworking. Therefore, for others to work at better levels of productivity, they must recognize you are empowering and enabling them to do their work. Educating them in how to do their work faster, better, cheaper, and more is important for all of you!

Interestingly, you can no longer be expected to be informed in all aspects of the work for which you are accountable. In other words, you are being asked to really manage and lead. And to manage and lead in today's workplace means you must know about the different educating approaches and when to use each one properly. In other words, you become a specialized generalist in managing and leading to assist the task specialists who work with you.

Importance of Learning

Some people benefit from online and/or face-to-face courses, workshops and seminars. However, most people learn through active participation in their immediate workspace.

One of the common denominators in every workplace is that everyone is involved in learning. In every moment, people are inundated with data. Sorting out the noise from the news involves learning about data filters and how to create useful information. Whoever is using educating approaches correctly is an asset to those learning about their filters and the creative process.

In the work-related learning and development revolution currently underway, it is a requirement to learn in better ways. Therefore, when you encourage others to share their knowledge and skills for the benefit of others, you've applied educating approaches that continue to grow and develop others. You've contributed to your managing and leading legacy.

Most enhancements you and others make in the work place, are made in the incidental moments in which all of you are working together. Little is solved if others are sent away to fill the knowing-doing gap in training seminars alone. It happens in the conversations. It happens in the mistakes. It happens in the questions.

Educating Approaches

The *9 educating approaches* identified in this book—with their accompanying definitions and brief introductions—are meant to differentiate among and yet connect the approaches you can use to engage the hands, heads, and hearts of others.

Learning and knowing how these 9 *educating approaches* are different, yet complementary, improves your ability to decide which approach—or combination of approaches—works for what situation.

Also, if your initial approach is not working, you have more options to draw from. One approach may work okay, but a combination of two or more may work even better.

Three examples:

1. To engage someone use coaching; use facilitating to draw ideas from them.
2. To retain involvement, use training for a new skill and mentoring for continued interest.
3. To improve performance, use career shifting and coaching because it may be more helpful to help the person leave the organization than to have them stay.

Through your words and follow-up actions, you will self-identify if others work with you, against you, or sit on the fence watching and waiting.

For situations where others are engaged and doing their best to support you, you must reflect on how they got to this point in their journey. You must identify how to do more of what works. *Remember – celebrate and appreciate; people will appreciate your gesture.*

For those situations where others are against you, ask yourself, "Is this the time for you to make a difference, or is it time to move on and let someone else help the group?" *Remember, you are not meant to handle every situation. Sometimes it is better for everyone to get out of the way.*

For those situations where others are sitting on the fence, you must figure out how best to get them involved. How can you engage their hands, heads, and hearts? *Remember, learning connects those willing to learn.*

Aside from observing others, you must learn what other managers and leaders know about their use of different educating approaches. For work-related learning and development to be significantly successful in any organization, all managers and leaders must be engaged in using educating approaches and sharing their stories about what is working.

You are encouraged to share what you know, rather than hoard.

Remember – you educate what you desire to learn.

Moving Forward

Having reached this point in the book, consider:

If your experience of managing and leading in work-related
learning and development has been confusing
and/or not up to the standard you desire,

then please read the learning outcomes that follow
to appreciate what the book can do for you
when you **Help Them Help YOU Manage-Lead**.

~~~~~~~~~

If your experience of managing, leading and
educating has been at the level you desire,
then read the learning outcomes below to develop a program
that will **Help Them Help YOU Manage-Lead** by educating
them in the 9 *educating approaches* that follow.

No matter what situation you find yourself in as a manager-leader, apply the 9 *educating approaches* to Help Them Help YOU Manage-Lead. In doing so, you will engage the hands, heads, and hearts of others in creating the well-living workplace. That is, you can manage and lead others to create a place of work where and when everyone works well together: A place of work where everyone likes what they do and does what they like.

It is IMPORTANT to use the educating practices that match the situations. One approach does not fit every situation.

Competencies

1.   Discuss the connection between managing and leading.
2.   Discuss the connection between educating and managing and leading.
3.   Define and discuss the terms 'learning', 'knowing' and 'educating.'
4.   Describe work-related learning and development.
5.   Discuss the connection between educating and work-related learning and development.
6.   Discuss an overall educating approach model.
7.   Discuss why the model is important to managing and leading.
8.   Define and discuss **instructing** and its contribution to learning and development.
9.   Define and discuss **training** and its contribution to learning and development.
10. Define and discuss **consulting** and its contribution to learning and development.
11. Value the connections among instructing, training, and consulting through the broader action of **teaching.**
12. Review and discuss three situations that involve training, consulting, and/or instructing.
13. Define and discuss **coaching** and its contribution to learning and development.
14. Define and discuss **shifting** and its contribution to learning and development.
15. Define and discuss **counselling** and its contribution to learning and development.
16. Value the connections among mentoring, shifting, and/or counselling through the broader action of **guiding.**
17. Review and discuss three situations that involve coaching, shifting, and counselling.
18. Define and discuss **facilitating** and its contribution to learning and development.
19. Define and discuss **mentoring** and its contribution to learning and development.
20. Define and discuss **minstrelling** and its contribution to learning and development.
21. Value the connections among facilitating, mentoring, and minstrelling through the broader action of **"saging" or educating.**
22. Review and discuss three situations that involve facilitating, coaching, and minstrelling.
23. Identify practical actions associated with each of the 9 educating approaches.
24. Discuss how educating approaches working as a whole support managing and leading in the workplace.
25. Review and discuss five examples that involve one or more of the *9 educating approaches* as a way to summarize learning.
26. Discuss the concept of 'courage to act through commitments.'

27. Value 9+1 suggestions for making and keeping commitments.
28. Value how the *9 educating approaches* encourage engagement.
29. Value how the *9 educating approaches* support retention.
30. Value how the *9 educating approaches* improve performance.
31. Value how the *9 educating approaches* contribute to managing-leading succession path.
32. Review and discuss the linkages between managing/leading and the 9 *educating approaches.*
33. Value which educating approaches are to be mastered for managing and those where you ask others to help you manage.
34. Value which educating approaches are to be mastered for leading and those where you ask others to help you lead.
35. Review an Action Mapping process to guide your transfer of learning.

Self Assessment of Competencies

As a way to gauge your current understanding of the contents of this book, review the competency list on the previous pages and self-assess your competence.

Today, can you (insert the competency statement) ... Yes or No?

From your responses, develop a topic awareness guideline for reading the book. Of the 35 competencies, which three to five require your attention as you move through the book?

Reflection:

Chapter 2:
Connecting Managing and Leading

Competency: Are you competent to ___ Yes or No:

1. Discuss the connection between managing and leading.

2. Discuss the connection between educating and managing-leading.

This chapter introduces the terms and concepts of management and leadership. Again, you are encouraged to seek additional content from other sources to add to this perspective.

Management, Managing, and Manager

Management is a body of knowledge. It is the "concepts and practices" you use to manage. In doing so, you are called a manager.

Therefore, as a manager you "have management." That is, you have access to a collection of concepts and practices, and tools and techniques to manage as a manager.

Specific examples of management concepts and practice are enfolded within titles like Performance Management, Knowledge Management, Systems Management, etc.

Managing is the action you take to apply your value of management. As you manage, you gain insight into your management decisions and how you manage. In addition, you gain feed-forward from the staff you manage.

Therefore, as a manager you "do managing or you manage"

The term manager is an organizational identifier used to describe when you manage while using the management concepts and practices the organization requires and requests of you. In addition, you weave into your practice what you determine is the best of what is available without conflicting with what your organization requires and requests.

Therefore, when applying management and managing, you are "being a manager" in support of organizational behaviour and development.

**To manage is to coordinate others through their motivation to achieve
the tactical plan, goals and objectives as set forth in the strategic map.
When you manage - you manage the systems for the people.**

Leadership, Leading, and Leader

Leadership is a body of knowledge. It is the "concepts and practices" you use to lead. In doing so, you are called a leader by those who follow you.

Therefore, as a leader you "have leadership." That is, you have access to a collection of concepts and practices, and tools and techniques to lead as a leader.

Specific examples of leadership theory and practice are enfolded under titles like Servant Leadership, Principle-Centred Leadership, Transformational Leadership, etc.

Leading is the action you take to apply your value of leadership. As you lead, you gain insight into your leadership decisions and how you lead. In addition, you gain feed-forward from the staff you lead.

Therefore, as a leader you "do leading or you lead"

The term leader is a gift given to you by those who follow you. The term is used to describe when you lead while using the leadership concepts and practices your followers require and request of you without conflicting with what your organization requires and requests of you.

Therefore, when applying leadership and leading, you are "being a leader" in the eyes of those who follow you.

**To lead is to influence each person through inspiration to attain,
And, where possible, exceed the intention of the
organizational mission, vision and values.
When you lead, you lead the person from his/her system.**

Two Sides of a Coin

Management/managing and leadership/leading are helpful in establishing or maintaining the organizations of systems and people in organizations." It is the content within each concept/practice that converts differently, yet complementarily, within the act of organizing systems and people according to the mission, vision and values identified by the organization.

That is, **Management and Leadership** are two sides of the same coin. You cannot have one without the other. However, when managing it is best to call it managing, and when leading, call it leading. To use the opposite term for the action experienced can be confusing for everyone involved.

On the next page, fill in the table to connect the matching activities for managing and leading. Suggested responses are provided in Appendix 1.

Two Examples Given in the Table:

When you manage, you tell or teach others what to do. When you lead, you guide or ask each person for their ideas.

Metaphorically, when you are managing, you position yourself on the dance floor so all you see is your dance partner and those close by. When you're leading, you are standing on the balcony and you see the whole dance floor. Managing is working in the system; leading is working on the system.

Mix and Match Key Connectors
Between Management and Leadership

Please fill in the empty boxes with corresponding words. Two examples are given.

Management, Managing, Manager	Leadership, Leading, Leader
Tell Others	Ask a Person
Dance Floor, Sitting Down, In	Balcony, Standing Up, On
Responsibility	X
X	Reflecting with Self
Innovation	X
Debriefing	X
Discussion and Debate	X
X	Inspiration
X	Recognition
Tactical Plan	X

*Suggested responses are provided in **Appendix 1**.

Chapter 2 Reflection

Having read Chapter 2, what are three insights you would draw from your learning? And why are they important to you today?

Insight 1 and its importance >

Insight 2 and its importance >

Insight 3 and its importance >

Chapter 3:
Connecting Educating with Managing and Leading

Competency: Are you competent to ___ Yes or No:

1. Discuss an overall educating approach model

2. Discuss why the model is important to managing and leading.

This Chapter connects the term educating with managing and leading.

Connecting Educating with Managing and Leading

Let's travel back in organizational development history and consider:

> *The answer was:*
> ***training***

> *The question was:*
> ***As a manager or leader, how do I help others others to help me manage and lead?***

At one time, training may have been the answer. However, in 21st century workplaces, training is not the answer——most of the time.

This observation highlights the next question:

In what ways might you involve others in being the best <u>for</u> the workplace?

Please add to the possible answers below.

1. Ask them share what they know about a topic at a meeting.

2. Conduct meetings where suggesting an improvement topic is on the agenda.

3. Recognize others for their learning and development.

4.

5.

6.

7.

Aside from the specific examples you listed above, consider three possible broad perspectives:

1. Management Learning Perspective

This perspective involves managers and leaders drawing from the principles, practices, and processes of management and leadership. They draw from the vast array of knowledge and skill possibilities they think and feel will help them to manage and lead.

In choosing, for example, one process (like conflict resolution) over another (like principle-centred negotiation), managers and leaders quickly learn that one managing/leading technique does not fit every situation. If that were the case, then every fastener used in house renovations would be a nail. It is widely known that there are as many types of fasteners as there are management and leadership tools and techniques.

2. Human Capital Perspective

This tactic involves managers and leaders asking the Human Resources or People Management department to intervene. This option involves assistance from others within and/or external to the organization. This approach leaves the managers and leaders to rely on someone else's know-why and know-how to get the work done with their staff.

Often, there is little or no transfer of learning for the manager and leader. Should they experience the situation again, they may have to bring someone back in again. Thus, staff may lose trust and respect for their manager-leader.

3. The Manager-Leader Uses Educating Approaches

This tactic involves managers and leaders using educating approaches appropriate for the work-related learning and development situation. That is, they help others learn how to deal with the situation and thereafter support others in their learning actions.

This procedure is similar to a rafting guide sitting in the back of the white water raft. This person has been with you from the beginning of the trip to the end. The guide offers insights into how to safely sit in the raft and effortlessly paddle the raft through the calm and white water sections of the river. The guide's intention is to ensure you have a great time, complete the journey safely, and leave with the satisfaction that "Wow, I did it," and "I will do this again and bring my friends along next time."

Educating Helps in YOUR Managing and Leading

There is an educator in every manager-leader.

Every day, you receive feedback from your efforts as a workplace educator. If your employees are doing it correctly, it's working! If they are not doing it correctly, review the situation and take corrective action using the *9 Educating Approaches*.

> If they (employees) go about their work in ways that are requested and required of them, then their work is accomplished.
>
> If they are constantly at your door wanting to know what to do next, then cost and time are impacted. Be sure not to take on their 'monkeys' as this action impacts your work. [A monkey is a task you accept that is the accountability of another person. For example, a new manager who reports to you, asks you how to fill in a lengthy form. You decide it's easier for you to do it now, than to show the new manager how to complete it.]

This sliding scale of 'others doing it themselves' and 'others want you to do it with them' (and sometimes doing it for them) are observed in the workplace every day.

You can appreciate people who are getting it correct. There are many tools and techniques to support the reward and recognition program.

For those situations where dialogue and action are incorrect, develop an intervention immediately. Small errors creeping into the work may unintentionally replicate. Thereafter, a negative ripple may affect the immediate and whole system until the error is found and corrected. Sooner is better than later. Using one or more of the educating approaches is a great way to frame the intervention.

Concern, however, is raised when your employees are constantly asking for your assistance. That means that you may not be doing the best for others in inspiring them to self-motivate. In other words, you are not helping them to help you manage and lead.

There is a 'blinking red light, noise making' concern felt when you end up doing the work for others. This action wreaks havoc for you, and it takes away from others doing their best for the organization. In such extreme cases, a toxic work situation is created because you do not have trust or confidence in the work of others.

Where are you on this scale?

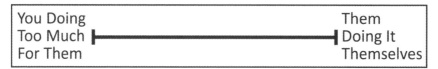

In response to this question, you have three tasks:
- Mark an '<' where you are now
- Mark an '>' where you will be 6 months from now.
- Between '< & >', is your learning-for-action.
  This book will help you achieve this.

<u>When they are doing it!</u>

For those situations where others are doing their own work, notice what you have been doing to help them accomplish this. Maybe you simply got out of the way; maybe you provided a welcome comment that included a helpful adaptation that sparked new work levels. Often it is the small things that matter.

<u>When You are - doing it!</u>

What about those situations which are not working so well? That is, you are sliding towards 'you doing too much for them'. What tools and techniques can you use to engage others? How do the chosen tools and techniques ensure that others will do the work and contribute to their personal well-being and the collective well-living of the group?

Metaphoric Connection

Here is a metaphoric example when offering first aid in the outdoors.

> In wilderness remote first aid situations, it is important for the first aider to ask themselves two important questions:
>
> 1. What do I see?
> 2. And why am I seeing it?
>
> From 'what do I see?' the first aider deals with the signs and symptoms, and provides care. From 'why am I seeing it?' the first aider deals with the cause, and provides care. Often the 'cause' is more important than the 'signs and symptoms.'

For example, a person is hiking in the mountains and stubs their toe on a rock, falls and starts crying. In asking the two questions stated above, you figure out:

>What I see: a stubbed toe.
>Why am I seeing it: It was caused by AMS (acute mountain sickness)
>The priority is AMS. That is the illness you treat!
>[By the way, to deal with AMS, descend, descend, descend!]

By extension, in your organizational life as a manager-leader, it is important to go beyond what you see to ask, "Why am I seeing it?"

>Example 1: People are arriving late to work. Why are they late?
>At first it may be a perception that they don't care.
>The real story may unfold like this:
>They have difficulty finding daycare that opens at a time that allows them to make it to work on time. Instead of mandating an 8:00 AM start, get them to start at 8:15, making up the 15 minutes throughout the day.

>Example 2: Of the people gossiping about restructuring, why are they gossiping?

>Example 3: Of the people absent every 6th or 7th Friday, why are they absent?

>Example 4: Of the people who are _____, why are they _____?

**If you can (first) figure out the 'why',
then you can figure out
the 'how' and 'who' that follows.**

Taking it a step further, consider the following two lists.

List #1: Evidence that something is not working for others:

1. Errors are repeated and may be increasing.
2. There is frustration in working with paradoxes such as 'do more with less'; this is confusing to them.
3. Trust is limited as employees are reluctant to work together or meetings are stalled.
4. Communication is sparse and it seems others are barking at one another.

5. Procedures are not followed.
6. Evaluation is inconsistent; sometimes it is done and the forms keep varying.
7. Performance criteria vary on many levels.
8. There is a lack of involvement in improving processes.
9. Fair exchange is not evident between what is said and what is done.
10. People are busy; however, their busyness is not contributing to the mission and vision of the organization.

Take each statement listed above and ask 'Why?' at least four to five times.

Reflect on this abbreviated example below, asking 'why' four times.
Key: M=manager, S=staff person:

Situation: Evaluation of work flow is inconsistent.

> M = Why is it inconsistent? >> S = Because we are using the old form.

> M = Why is the old form a problem? >> S = Because that is what you keep giving to us with that stupid manual.

> M = Why is the manual stupid? >> S = Because it is written in words that don't make sense.

> M = Why do the words stop you from using the manual >> S = Because I do not understand it, and I feel stupid. I wish you would just tell me, rather than me having to read this stuff.

> M = If someone were to offer training in how to fill out the form would that help? >> S = Yes.

> M = Would it help if we developed a job aid – a short cut to using the manual?
> S = You bet!

> M = Consider it done. This Friday okay? ...

List #2: Evidence that things are working for others:

It's helpful to ask 'why' at the end of each statement._

1. Fun and laughter are experienced each day because people feel at ease with one another.
2. People arrive on time to meetings.
3. People willingly stay after work to finish the task.
4. People get involved in volunteer activities.
5. People do not use sarcasm.
6. People ask questions in meetings to clarify points.
7. We use dialogue rather than debate in our meetings.

What are three statements you can add to the list above?

8. _____
9. _____
10. _____

Of the two lists mentioned above, which one inspires and motivates you? →

#1 __   #2__

Which list would engage the hands, heads, and hearts of others? →

#1 __   #2__

Managing and Leading and Learning

At the end of management and leadership workshops, teleseminars, and coaching sessions, a question often asked is:

**What can I do to deal with situations where there is
evidence of something not working for others?**

It is an important question.

However, this 'glass is half-empty' question and its ensuing perspective may not turn the situation in your favour in ways that benefit you and everyone involved.

A far more significant question is:

**What can I do to increase situations where there is
evidence that things are working?**

This 'glass is half-full' question and perspective offer you a new framework
to work through and a new platform from which to leap "fromward".
Fromward=what you are working from, what you manifest (vision) to materialize
(outcomes).

To begin to answer this reformatted question, here are three important tasks:

First, *be aware of* **what is happening in your working relationship with those
you manage and lead.**

1.   Are you doing it with them?
2.   Are you helping them to do it?
3.   Are you helping them to help you do it?
4.   Are you helping them to help you manage and/or lead as they do it?

In your observation, remember:

Whatever a person does, it serves them somehow—including you!

Learn how people's actions (behaviour or non-behaviour) serve them.

Second, *be attentive to* **what is working well and what can be improved upon.
In other words, what is hindering and helping others in doing their jobs, and
what is hindering and helping you in managing and leading?**

You can personally carry out this assessment and share your findings with
others (employees?) and see if they agree. In some situations where there is
mutual trust, this approach may work well.

A better approach is to engage others in assessing what is happening and draw
insights into how everyone could improve the workplace.

Either way, shine your light on what is happening. You can look out for what
is helping and what is hindering but be careful not to stay in the 'what is
hindering' perspective and fix things. However, if the problem is affecting
things NOW, then action may be needed NOW. If a person is using a tool
incorrectly, then a fix is needed immediately. If a person continually submits
a weekly report without all of the information, then corrections are needed.
If a person—from your perspective—is not listening well, sending them on a
training course called 'Listening 101' may not be the best solution. The issue

may have as much to do with you as the person who thinks the other is not listening.

As you plan to move forward with action, consider:

> What will you continue doing?
> What will you start doing?
> What will you stop doing?

Third, **_be intentional in_ carrying out activities and following through on planned actions that contribute to others engaging more in the workplace. It is helpful if you share your intentions with others.**

Engage, enable, empower, and help others to envisage something more for themselves individually and collectively.

As a manager-leader, it is important for you to become competent in the ways and means of engaging the hands, heads, and hearts of others. Learning about managing and leading is an ever-improving story.

Bring It Together

Your experience of engagement will be directly proportionate to fulfilling your commitments.

1. Continue doing what works; make sure you do it.
2. Stop doing what is not helping; stop doing it NOW.
3. Start doing it!

And in all of what you do, remember:

Help Them Help YOU Manage-Lead

9 Educating Approaches

At the heart of this book are the 9 *educating approaches* that support managing and leading. These nine approaches were gleaned from years of reading, writing, and consulting practice observing what was and what was not working when managers and leaders were engaging others.

Four of the approaches link with managing just as four of them link with leading. And one of the four from managing and one from leading also combine with a third approach to form a higher level platform.

The following figure highlights the nine approaches in relationship to one another.

The next figure highlights the nine approaches in relationship to managing and leading. Additional connections are made and explained after presentation of the diagram.

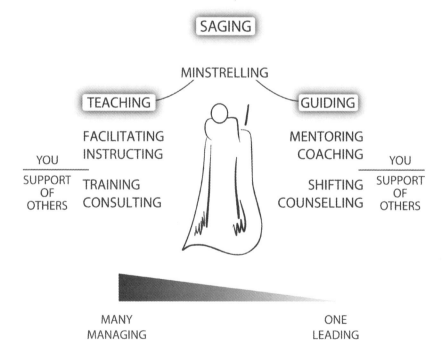

Additional Explanations Applicable to the Figure Above

The reference to 'You' and 'Support of Others' suggests that when you lead it is important for you to know how to coach and mentor. Also, you need to know enough about shifting (career development) and counselling to help connect people whom you are guiding with people who can better support them. Similarly, when you manage, it is important to know how to facilitate and instruct while knowing whom to ask for assistance in training and consulting.

The reference to the sliding scale of one and many highlights the idea that when you lead you usually deal with one person, whereas when you manage you are dealing with many. However, it is possible to coach many, just as it is possible to facilitate one.

On the managing side, you phrase the work as dealing with problems that require resolution. Therefore, you use problem inquiry. On the leading side, you phrase the work as dealing with appreciations that require expansion. Therefore, you use appreciative inquiry. These additional insights add to the table introduced in Chapter 2, page 34.

Chapter 3 Reflection

Having read Chapter 3, what are three insights you would draw from your learning? And why are they important to you today?

Insight 1 and its importance >

Insight 2 and its importance >

Insight 3 and its importance >

Chapter 4:
Work-Related Learning and Development, and Educating

Competency: Are you competent to ___ Yes or No:

1. Define and discuss the terms 'learning', 'knowing' and 'educating.'

2. Describe work-related learning and development.

3. Connect educating with work-related learning and development.

This chapter introduces you to the terms and concepts *learning, knowing,* and *educating* and connects workplace educating with the concept of work-related learning and development.

What follows is not meant to be a definitive, all encompassing presentation on the three terms and concepts. Rather, these key terms are introduced as an awakening, of sorts, from which you can springboard onto the 9 *educating approaches*. These educating approaches are then linked with managing and leading, which aims to:

Help Them Help YOU Manage-Lead

Learning

Here are three historical perspectives on learning:

> Learning is the center of our ability to adapt to the most trivial and the most profound situational demands. It makes the difference between purposeful action and directionless activity.
> ~ West, Farmer and Wolff (1991)

> Learning is a relatively permanent change in behaviour or behavioural potentiality that comes from experience and cannot be attributed to temporary body states such as illness, fatigue, or drugs.
> ~ Hergenhahn and Olsen (1993)

> Learning is about detecting and correcting errors.
> ~ Argyris and Schon (1996)

Learning is the gaining of understanding about something. It is connected with psychology (study of the psyche or consciousness) moving towards philosophy. It involves the connection among finding facts, collecting data, and creating information.

Learning can be used as a noun, verb or adjective in the English language:
- The <u>learning</u> taken from the workshop was helpful.
      << noun linked with knowledge
- The manager was <u>learning</u> about leadership today.
      << verb linked with to learn leadership
- The senior executive views the company as a <u>learning</u> organization.
      << adjective

Knowing

Here are two historical perspectives on knowing, more commonly referred to as knowledge:

Explicit or codified knowledge refers to knowledge that is transmittable in formal, systematic language. On the other hand, tacit knowledge has a personal quality, which makes it hard to formalize and communicate.
~ Nonaka (1994)

Knowledge is information combined with experience, context, interpretation, and reflection. It is a high-value form of information that is ready to apply to decisions and actions.
~ Davenport et al. (1998)

Knowing is having a comprehension of something. Connected with philosophy (study of value, truth, worth, utility), it involves the connection among creating information, generating knowledge, and sharing wisdom

Knowing refers to 'knowing that' (theory – *a priori* (beforehand) = product) and 'knowing how' (task – *a posteriori* (afterwards) = process).

In combination, learning allows for knowing, as knowing allows for learning. That is, you cannot have one without the other when you are consciously attuned to their presence as both product and process.

Educating

Here are two historical perspectives on educating and education:

> Education is life—not a mere preparation for an unknown kind of future living.
>> ~ Lindeman (1926)

> Education: To educate ... is to guide [learners] on an inner journey toward more truthful ways of seeing and being the world.
>> ~ Palmer (1998)

Formal education occurs when society, a group, or individuals set up a programme of study to educate people (often associated with the 'students' in schools, colleges and universities). Organizations develop, bring educators in, and/or send employees out for formal training and development programs.

Formal education can become systematic and thorough. Formal education systems can be used to promote ideals or values as well as knowledge.

> Help persons become great citizens and/or great employees ... *teach* them from the outside in.

Adult education has become established and is often branded as 'adult learning' or 'lifelong learning.' It is also known as workplace learning or work-related learning and development within organizations.

Adult education takes on many forms from organized learning (like workshops and seminars) to self-organized learning (incidental or situational learning).

> Help persons become who they choose to become ... *guide* them from the inside out.

The use of the terms *teaching* and *guiding* here are purposeful; this will become more evident in the following Chapters.

Educating with Learning and Knowing

Educating fosters and fashions the connections between learning and knowing. That is, educating supports the system of: fact finding, data collection, information creation, knowledge generation, and wisdom sharing where wisdom shared is new facts for others and for you.

Also, educating is about combining teaching and guiding approaches that help persons become great citizens through deciding whom they choose to become. Teaching and guiding complement the learning and knowing that occurs.

For adults in the workplace—your staff—numerous ways of learning and knowing are available for which, through which, and from which you can engage their hands, heads, and hearts using the 9 *educating approaches* outlined in this book.

**Learning for knowing, or
learning how to learn for knowing how to action,
is at the foundation of work
(performance improvement).**

**Educating uses tools and techniques
to build and grow the work
(performance increases productivity).**

Educating and Work-Related Learning and Development

Unfortunately, many people in the workplace have a negative association with education. They may go so far as to think their learning stopped when they finished high school. Some people have turned down or turned off their learning.

To live one's great life and contribute to the well-living workplace means learning and knowing are involved in every moment; they are constant companions.

The workplace is where work-related learning occurs. For the amount of time people spend in the workplace, it's important that workplace learning and development are a rich experience for them.

Broadly defined, there are three types of work-related learning situations:

> 1) Incidental: within the sphere of current work [in the moment]
>
> 2) Informal: away from the sphere of current work [learner identified]
>
> 3) Formal: away from the sphere of current work [organization identified]

Incidents, or work-related learning events, can bring mistakes or success to the forefront. Mistakes are often particularly insightful. Learning can be rich and alive and leveraged for the next situation. Similarly, success can be debriefed and key learning-for-knowing used for the next situation.

Action could be formal and/or informal. Formal in the sense that you will participate in work-related learning and development as set out by the organization. This action will be helpful now. Informal action has you looking for work-related learning and development opportunities outside or inside the organization, as determined by you. This action will be helpful later.

> Situations to consider:
>
> If errors reoccur and/or low productivity rates result, often learning has not been internalized for that person and/or group. In other words, that person/group is not developing at a level that meets the organization identified job competencies. Such situations require that more determined formal learning opportunities be identified and made available - sometimes at the expense of informal learning opportunities.
>
> However, not all learning is aligned with mistakes. There is also success at work that must be celebrated. This learning is rich, and we recognize what works best and that doing more of it contributes to productivity and performance.

When you use your knowledge and skills of learning, knowing, and educating, you have more ways in which to help others live their great lives while creating the well-living workplace.

Chapter 4 Reflection

Having read Chapter 4, what are three insights you would draw from your learning? And why are they important to you today?

Insight 1 and its importance >

Insight 2 and its importance >

Insight 3 and its importance >

Chapter 5:
Teaching = Teach on the Reach

Competency: Are you competent to ___ Yes or No:

1. Define and discuss instructing and its contribution to work-related learning and development.

2. Define and discuss training and its contribution to work-related learning and development.

3. Define and discuss consulting and its contribution to work-related learning and development.

4. Value the connections among training, consulting and instructing through the broader action of teaching.

5. Review and discuss three workplace situations that involve training, consulting and/or instructing.

6. Identify practical actions associated with training, consulting and instructing.

MINSTRELLING

TEACHING

FACILITATING

INSTRUCTING

TRAINING

CONSULTING

MENTORING

COACHING

SHIFTING

COUNSELLING

Discovering instructing, training, and consulting

Please read the story that follows.

Whitewater Rafting: A Metaphor

Looking up, 'Hobbit' saw his rafting crew walking towards him. They had just finished their safety talk with the trip leader. They were now joining him for their trip down the river. A mixed group in age and size, they seemed to be made up of two families. One group appeared to be a dad and two teenage children. The second group had a mum, dad, and two younger children.

The dad with the teenagers seemed nervous. After 20 years of working as a white-water rafting guide, Hobbit had a sense for where people are coming from.

"Hi and welcome. My name is Hobbit – my river name," he said smiling. "So you're my crew today! Welcome!"

"As the trip leader said, I will give you some instructions on how to paddle. And I will make sure you know how to sit in the boat so you can maximize the ride with the minimum amount of effort. Sound good?"

There were enthusiastic nods from the family of three, less so from the family of four.

"How many of you have rafted before?" Hobbit asked, scanning the group.

The group of three who stood to the left of the raft said they had rafted on the Kananaskis River last summer.

"How was that trip?" asked Hobbit moving slightly towards the group of three.

The father said, "Great! We had a great time." Patting his hand on his son's head, "Jacob wanted to go again – sooner than later! So we thought we would step it up a notch. Is that what we are going to do? I heard this river can be high this time of year."

"Sure, we can do that. So are you looking for the rock, the roll, or a rock and roll trip?" Hobbit asked with a Cheshire cat smile.

The family enthusiastically nodded yes while the other family standing on the other side of the raft seemed even quieter.

Turning to the four, and moving towards them around the front of the raft, Hobbit said "Come on! No worries. I'll share some ways to have a great day. And I'll make sure you know how to paddle before we hit anything bigger than what you see here. By the time you make it through the first big rapid, you'll be wondering why the fuss?"

"So what brought you here today?"

"It's my birthday tomorrow!" said the teenage girl looking at her dad. "I've wanted to do this since my friend told me it was a blast. Is that true?" she asked, turning her attention to Hobbit.

"Ya bet-ya! It's great! And, happy birthday." There were smiles from everyone.

Looking at the Dad, "You seem a little quiet or nervous. Is there a reason?" asked Hobbit.

He said, "Seems ridiculous, but I don't know how to swim."

"No problems. The life jacket will keep you afloat, which is a great lead to me sharing a few things that can help you to stay in the raft. Fair enough?

"Sure!"

Moving to the front of the raft, Hobbit picked up his paddle, and said "Let's start with paddle strokes I need from you. I'll need you to paddle forward and backward." After his demonstration, he asked everyone to pick up the paddles they had brought with them. They all practiced what Hobbit showed them. "I only ask for those strokes because I use the river to do a lot of my work."

"As to sitting in the raft, the best way to have fun today is to maintain three points of contact. First, put your butt on the outside tube. Next, wedge your foot/feet under the boat tube you are sitting on or the one in front," Hobbit was demonstrating the positions, "and your paddle in the water. Give up one of those points of contact, and you will be at the mercy of the raft and river. That is when you will have an 'inside out experience'. The paddle works as a third point of contact because when you paddle, you apply pressure on the water. It keeps you sitting upright."

What does this story have to do with instructing, training, and consulting?

Please read ahead, and return afterwards to identify where one or more of the 3 educating approaches identified and discussed in this chapter are found in this story.

Instructing

To instruct is to provide a description and explanation of the knowledge and skill at a deeper level.

- An instructor supports participants in learning the knowledge and associated skills of a collection of connected topics.

- An instructor ensures the knowledge (with the skill) is learned to a predetermined level.
- An instructor has a vested interest in participants learning about the 'Why and Who' for use in the future rather than the immediate 'How' of the topic for use immediately.

An often heard statement from participants involved in an instructional event:

"I need to know that by understanding why."

Can you think of two examples where you might <u>instruct</u> others in your workplace?

1.

2.

Training

To train is to impart some particular skill with some knowledge for immediate use.
A trainer transmits to participants what they need to know about how to do a skill.
A trainer ensures the 'How' skill is learned to a predetermined level.
A trainer has a vested interest in participants meeting specified criteria for immediate use.

An often heard statement from participants involved in a training event:

"I do not know how to do it."

Can you think of two examples where you might <u>train</u> others in your workplace?

1.

2.

Consulting

To consult is to provide information and/or to exchange ideas based on inquiries with someone else.

- A consultant provides support to participants in solving a problem identified by the participants.
- A consultant shares or enquires after knowledge in content, process, or construct.
- A consultant has a vested interest in achieving the correct results as determined through the consultant's dialogue with participants.

An often heard statement from participants involved in a consulting event:

"I do not know what I know; You do. Help us!"

Can you think of two examples where you might <u>consult</u> for others in your workplace?

1.

2.

Quick Reminder

MINSTRELLING

TEACHING

FACILITATING   MENTORING

INSTRUCTING   COACHING

TRAINING   SHIFTING

CONSULTING   COUNSELLING

Worksheet for Teaching

Deciding on an Educating Approach:
The Approach Complements the Situation

As previously mentioned, when managing and leading others it is important to select an educating approach that works best for the situation.

Consider the three examples listed below and identify which of the 3 educating approach(es) would work best for each situation.

Remember:

Instructing: To instruct is to provide a description and explanation of the knowledge and/or skill at a deeper level.

Training: To train is to impart some particular skill with some knowledge for use immediately.

Consulting: To consult is to provide information and/or to exchange ideas based on inquiries with someone else.

Example 1:

10 new recruits were hired on Tuesday to support the *call-out program*, informing past clients of the new products and services offered by the company after the recent merger. New phone systems with hands-free features were installed on Monday.

Which approach(es) would be the most appropriate for the above example:

Instructing   Training Consulting

→   Why?

Example 2:

Three recently promoted group managers approached you with an employee engagement issue from their work area.

Which approach(es) would be the most appropriate for the above example:

Instructing   Training Consulting

→   Why?

Example 3:

Two emergent leaders from another part of the organization asked you to lunch to discuss the roll-out of the new principle-centred negotiation program you developed for project management in international settings. They have had limited success in implementing the program in their African operations. They are in for two days of attending meetings and emailed you to set up the four-hour meeting.

Which approach(es) would be most appropriate for the above example:

Instructing   Training Consulting

→   Why?

See Appendix 1 for suggested responses.

Possible Actions for Teaching

Instructing: To instruct is to provide a description and explanation of the knowledge and skill at a deeper level.
- Develop an outline of terms and concepts to be learned by your staff Share the outline and the path for learning.
- Identify the most critical and important skills each person needs to demonstrate to do their job.
- Set aside time at meetings to answer 'Why, Who, How' questions.

Two Additional Actions:

1.

2.

Training: To train is to impart some particular skill with some knowledge for immediate use.
- Set up a regular time to show staff how to complete the task with time to practice before giving them the green light to proceed.
- Determine when a training intervention is required for a person, and explain why the person will be sent on training. (In taking this action, determine if training or managing is the best response to the question "How can I ensure this person is competent?")
- Find people who are doing things correctly and thank them. When they are not doing them correctly, provide trainable (teachable) moments to get them back on track.

Two Additional Actions:

1.

2.

Consulting: To consult is to provide information and/or to exchange ideas.
- Set aside time at meetings to address one positive or negative issue Where it is negative, seek a solution; where it is positive, seek to do more of it.
- Find out what your staff members know: with some creative and innovative review, you may find hidden talents in your staff that can support the work at hand.
- Determine when a consulting intervention is required for the project and explain why another person will be supporting the project for the time specified. (In taking this action, determine whether consulting or

your leveraging of staff knowledge and skill is the best response to the question "How can I ensure the project is completed correctly?")

Two Additional Actions:

1.

2.

Return to the rafting story at the beginning of this chapter, and identify where *instructing, training,* and *consulting* might apply.

Chapter 5 Reflection

Having read Chapter 5, what are three insights you would draw from your learning? And why are they important to you today?

Insight 1 and its importance >

Insight 2 and its importance >

Insight 3 and its importance >

For further tips, tools, and techniques about the 9 educating approaches visit:
www.managingleading.com/cpages/9educating-approaches

Chapter 6:
Guiding = Guide on the Ride

Competency: Are you competent to ___ Yes or No:

1. Define and discuss **coaching** and its contribution to work-related learning and development.

2. Define and discuss **shifting** and its contribution to work-related learning and development.

3. Define and discuss **counselling** and its contribution to work-related learning and development.

4. Identify practical actions associated with coaching, shifting and counselling.

5. Review and discuss three examples that involve coaching, shifting and/or counselling.

6. Consider the connections among coaching, shifting and counselling through the broader action of guiding.

MINSTRELLING

GUIDING

FACILITATING
INSTRUCTING
TRAINING
CONSULTING

MENTORING
COACHING
SHIFTING
COUNSELLING

Discovering coaching, shifting, and counselling

Please read the story that follows.

Whitewater Rafting Story Continues

It was the second day of the trip, and everyone was feeling comfortable with the raft and what they had to do. The fun and singing the night before led everyone to connect as though they were lost family members uniting after a few years apart. The teenagers babysat the younger children, leaving the parents to chat and tell hilarious stories of their adventures and work.

Mixed in with the laughter were the stories told by the other guides. Occasionally, Hobbit shared some stories of his 20+ years of guiding. Most of the time, he smiled and encouraged others to tell their stories.

The parents of the younger children, Jan and Herbert, noticed how Hobbit would engage with the single dad, Jonathan. They seemed to have sidebar conversations where Jonathan would speak and Hobbit would ask another question. Jonathan seemed into the conversation as he turned his body to hear Hobbit a little better. At least, that is how it appeared to them because Jonathan kept nodding his head like he finally understood something that had been puzzling him.

Jan and Herbert were also impressed when Hobbit took their children on a nature walk. They held back from fully engaging as Hobbit gave the children insights about the bush that they had not known before. The amazing thing about the walk and talk was how he wove their story of becoming teenagers into the nature examples he shared. The kids were enthralled as were Jan and Herbert. They knew he must have worked with children before.

Noticing Hobbit get up from the table, Herbert approached him and asked if he could chat.

"You seem to enjoy your work," Herbert said to Hobbit as they walked towards the river.

"You bet – best summer job I have had. Don't do as much now as I used to. I have a company to run."

"So this is not your primary job?"

"No. I'm an entrepreneur involved in an international education-based company that I co-founded."

Herbert seemed a little surprised. Hobbit could see it in his eyes.

Hobbit had seen that look many times after sharing what else he did for a living when people asked. as he rarely introduced what he did besides rafting. He was the CEO of a million dollar company doing business in various parts of the world. He rafted as a way to escape the city and to meet great people like Jan, Herbert, Jonathan, and the kids.

"That's interesting. I work as a leadership coach," Herbert said as they started down the steps to the staging area for today's rafting trip.
"Yes, I remember you mentioning that yesterday," Hobbit commented as they reached the end of the steps. "Do you enjoy what you do?"

"Well, yes and no. I am looking to try new things. I want to begin teaching at a college. I have just finished my master's degree, and I have a friend at the community college that can get me on as a part-time instructor in the business department."

"Did that as well," Hobbit chuckled. "A great place to wet your whiskers," said Hobbit scratching his chin.

What does this story have to do with mentoring, shifting, and counselling?

Please read ahead, and return afterwards to identify where one or more of the three educating approaches identified and discussed in this Chapter are found in this story.

Coaching

To coach is to drive and/or urge participation through the task.

- A coach encourages the most from participants without actually doing whatever needs to be done.

- A coach helps participants do it, for they are the ones charged with doing it.

- A coach has a vested interest in heartening the participants to be the best for their work.

An often heard statement from participants involved in coaching:

"I know what I know. I am not sure I can do it alone."

What are two examples of where you might coach someone in your workplace?

1.

2.

Shifting

To shift is to support understanding of personal career decisions.

- A shifter supports participants in realizing their life map by appealing to participants' hierarchy of values and vocation decisions.

- A shifter assists in the identification of what challenges are to be placed in front of participants to help the participants with their learning and development.

- A shifter has a vested interest in connecting career decisions with life purpose.

An often heard statement from participants involved in shifting:

**"I am unsure of what I need to
know to meet my career decisions."**

Can you think of two examples where you might <u>shift</u> someone in your workplace?

1.

2.

Counselling

To counsel is to talk things over and to listen with caring.

- A counsellor empathetically assists participants to reach a plane of reflection.

- A counsellor wants participants to reach a place of self-acceptance.

- A counsellor has a vested interest in unblocking what participants identify as the issue.

An often heard statement from participants involved in counselling:

**"I know something is holding me back.
Help me understand the situation."**

Can you think of two examples where you might <u>counsel</u> someone in your workplace?

1.

2.

Quick Reminder

MINSTRELLING

GUIDING

FACILITATING

INSTRUCTING

TRAINING

CONSULTING

MENTORING

COACHING

SHIFTING

COUNSELLING

Worksheet for Guiding

Deciding on an Educating Approach:
The Approach Complements the Situation

When managing and leading others, it is important to select an educating approach that works best for the situation.

Consider the three examples listed below and identify which of the 3 educating approach(es) would work best for each situation.

Coaching: To coach is to provide trusted advice during the adventure.

Shifting: To shift is to support understanding of personal career directions.

Counselling: To counsel is to talk things over and to listen with caring.

Example 1:

Friday, mid-afternoon, you notice Mary-Jane slumped over her desk. She looks exhausted. When you ask her what is happening, she says her two college aged children are coming in for the weekend and she is not ready. She hasn't done the shopping or cleaned the house. She has been working overtime all week. As Mary-Jane's manager, you wonder how you can help her.

Which approach(es) would be most appropriate for the above example:

      Coaching   Shifting   Counselling

    →   Why?

Example 2:

A long-term client has complained about the service he has received over the past six months. He is willing to give you another chance before pulling the account. He enjoys working with you because you hold him accountable for his actions. However, he has voiced displeasure with the paperwork he has to complete. Also, he mentioned he seems to get lost in the shuffle. He is not computer savvy and freely admits that point.

Which approach(es) would be most appropriate for the above example:

      Coaching   Shifting   Counselling

    →   Why?

Example 3:

For many weeks now, Eileen has been sharing her love for web design. During the past year, she has been studying in the evenings at a community college. On recent numerous occasions, she has voiced her displeasure about her job. As the mid-level manager of the consulting company for which she works, you heard her tell her story again at lunch.

Which approach(es) would be most appropriate for the above example:

      Coaching   Shifting   Counselling

      →   Why?

See **Appendix 1** for suggested responses.

Possible Actions for Guiding

Coaching: To coach is to drive and/or urge participation through the task.
- Create a spontaneous relationship with your staff, employing a style that is open, flexible and confident.
- Identify what trust means to both of you before engaging in coaching
- Demonstrate respect for staff's perceptions, learning styles, and personal well-being as each person you coach is unique.

Two Additional Actions:

1.

2.

Shifting: To shift is to support understanding of personal career decisions.
- Ask your staff what is important to them in their lives as a whole and their work in particular; seek to understand their hierarchy of values
- What do they value in their lives? Support them in working with those values.
- Explore the challenges blocking your staff's career growth and celebrate what is encouraging them to move ahead; knowing what encourages them will help them overcome challenges. Find ways to do more of it.
- Encourage your staff to participate in a personal values, vision and life purpose workshop so they might understand more about themselves. It is helpful if you model the way.

Two Additional Actions:

1.

2.

Counselling: To counsel is to talk things over and to listen with caring.
- Listen with an empathetic ear to what is happening in your staff's lives. If necessary, direct them to those within the organization who can assist them.
- Celebrate the milestones in people's lives like birthdays and promotions.
- Discuss work-related issues. When and where you can, encourage them to respond rather than react. Help them to anticipate and prevent more issues.

Two Additional Actions:

1.

2.

Return to the rafting story at the beginning of the Chapter, and identify where *mentoring, shifting, and counselling* might apply.

Chapter 6 Reflection

Having read Chapter 6, what are three insights you would draw from your learning? And why are they important to you today?

Insight 1 and its importance >

Insight 2 and its importance >

Insight 3 and its importance >

For further tips, tools, and techniques about the 9 educating approaches visit: www.managingleading.com/cpages/9educating-approaches

Chapter 7:
Sage = Sage off the Page

Competency: Are you competent to ___ Yes or No:

1. Define and discuss **facilitating** and its contribution to work-related learning and development.

2. Define and discuss **mentoring** and its contribution to work-related learning and development.

3. Define and discuss **minstrelling** and its contribution to work-related learning and development.

4. Review and discuss three examples that involve facilitating, mentoring and/or minstrelling.

5. Identify practical actions associated with facilitating, mentoring and minstrelling.

6. Consider the connections among facilitating, mentoring, and minstrelling through the broader action of **"saging" or educating**.

Discovering facilitating, mentoring, and minstrelling

Please read the story that follows.

Whitewater Rafting: A Metaphor

"Okay, what would you like to do today?" Hobbit stood before the group who were all dressed and ready to take on the second day of rafting—a day filled with bigger holes and bigger waves (rapids?). He had just explained that he would teach them how to guide the raft. The kids said "Sure!" Herbert was for it. Jan and Jonathan stood back a little.

"I want the full trip," Janine squealed, seemingly vibrating with happiness. "It's my birthday and I want to go for it!"

"Maybe we should start with a birthday dunk. What do you say Janine?" With that, she ran behind her dad smilingly.

"Maybe later!" Hobbit said, winking at Herbert.

Turning to Jonathan, Hobbit said, "You mentioned last night that you were going to take on a risk this week. How about helping me guide this morning?"

"Um … yea, okay. Why not? I'm game!"

"Great." Stepping closer to the raft, Hobbit picked up his paddle and said, "Well, let's get going. Oh yea! Do you need me to go over the paddling strokes or commands?"

Everyone shook their head no.

"Okay, well pick her up and let's get going."

****

Jonathan was doing a great job in the back. He was feeling at ease helping Hobbit. It seemed he opened up a lot and was joking around with everyone. He learned the commands and encouraged everyone to do their bit.

Because he was learning so quickly, Hobbit let him take the raft through a grade two stretch of water. They made it through safely, with Jonathan sharing high fives with his kids.

"Around the corner is where we are stopping for a quick lunch. I have sandwiches and drinks in the bag." Hobbit was pointing at the red water tight bag in the middle of the raft.

****

Hobbit's group stopped for a break alongside the other rafting group. Hobbit sensed that something was up.

"So what's up, everyone?"

Jan spoke first. "We were all chatting about our experience. Remember yesterday when you took the kids on that nature walk and you connected nature to them becoming teenagers? I was wondering if you could share some thoughts about rafting and working. You seemed to have some wonderful insights that would be fun to hear. And you were so quiet last night."

"Sure. Is that okay with everyone?"

The adults nodded more enthusiastically than the kids. Yet everyone turned and faced Hobbit as they munched on their sandwiches.

"Let me ask, what have you learned from being on the trip about living your great life or creating a place of work where you love what you do and do what you love?"

What does this story have to do with facilitating, mentoring, and minstrelling?

Please read ahead, and return afterwards to identify where one or more of the 3 educating approaches identified and discussed in this Chapter are found in this story.

Facilitating

To facilitate is to help a process go well, to draw out from the person/people blue-sky ideas.

- A facilitator draws responses from participants in a setting conducive to their need for learning.

- A facilitator oversees the process for participants to learn what they need to do.

- A facilitator has a vested interest in helping the participants to get to a place of decision-making for action.

An often heard statement from participants involved in a facilitated event:

"I do not know that I do not know."

List two examples of where you might <u>facilitate</u> others in your workplace?

1.

2.

Mentoring

To mentor is to provide trusted advice during the adventure.

- A mentor speaks the truth of experience when participants are most likely ready to listen.

- A mentor shares experiences in a causal way.

- A mentor has a vested interest in participants gaining insight about themselves by sharing the lived experience of the mentor.

An often heard statement from participants who are being mentored:

**"I know I am stuck. With your experience, you can
advise me to see what I'm missing or need to know."**

Can you think of two examples where you might mentor someone in your workplace?

1.

2.

Minstrelling

To minstrel is to reconcile the other eight educating types through storytelling and fostering the natural rhythms of learning and educating.

A minstrel shares a path of learning with participants that seeks balance for knowing infinitely.

A minstrel identifies **NEWS** of the day and shares it willingly and mindfully - where news arrives from the four directions - North, East, West and South.

A minstrel has a vested interest in sharing paths to knowing that promote, embrace, and integrate what is learned with what is known about living from the future-based intentions.

An often heard statement from participants involved in minstrelling:

"I know I have something to share with others."

What are two examples of where you might become a <u>minstrel</u> in your workplace?

1.

2.

Quick Reminder

Worksheet for Saging

Deciding on an Educating Approach:
The Approach Complements the Situation

When managing and leading others, it is important to select an educating approach that works best for the situation.

Consider the three examples listed below and identify which of the 3 educating approach(es) would work best for each situation.

Facilitating: To facilitate is to help a process go well, to draw out from the person/people blue-sky-ideas.

Mentoring: To mentor is to provide trusted advice during the adventure.

Minstrelling: To minstrel is to reconcile the other eight educating types through storytelling and fostering the natural rhythms of learning and educating.

Example 1:

Jonathan is a senior engineer who is well-liked by his colleagues. In about two months, he will be transferring to the Hawaiian office where he will retire in another three years. He has a wealth of knowledge and skill that he is willing to share with a few colleagues. He has said he is willing to 'hold court,' a term he affectionately uses to describe the 'time spent sharing' his thoughts with the younger engineers.

Which approach(es) would be most appropriate for the above example:

       Facilitating   Mentoring   Minstrelling

    →   Why?

Example 2:

Joshua, a Gen-Xer, is a recent master's graduate in leadership who has been working in your unit for the past six months. He is a little brash at times, and he has made it known he wants to move on. During your bi-weekly coffee with him yesterday, he mentioned an opening was available in the parent company office. He is seeking some advice.

Which approach(es) would be most appropriate for the above example:

       Facilitating   Mentoring   Minstrelling

    →   Why?

Example 3:

You have been hired to reorganize a department in a Caribbean resort. For the past two years, the department has received low ratings from its staff and the clients have been commenting on declining service quality. Some clients have gone so far as to say they will not be returning. Next Tuesday is your first day.

Which approach(es) would be most appropriate for the above example:

      Facilitating   Mentoring   Minstrelling

→   Why?

Possible Actions for "Saging"

Facilitating: To facilitate is to help a process go well, to encourage blue sky ideas

- Notice your involvement with the group when you encourage their ideas and input. Are you standing at the front or sitting among them? Is someone recording or are you? Are you supporting the process or the outcome as you facilitate?

- Use various ways to draw responses from participants, including wading through the silence of the question you ask. Let them respond somehow and then engage with them.

- Explain the decision-making format that will align with the action needed. Majority voting is not the answer in every situation.

Two Additional Actions:

      1.

      2.

Mentoring: To mentor is to provide trusted advice during the adventure.   →

- Hold a monthly meeting with each of your direct reports, and ask them what they need to be the best for the organization – listen and then share your thoughts.Consider the comments you make to each person you mentor. Are you being casual – taking the person somewhere, to do something? Are you casual – e.g., engaging in a light hearted approach to sharing advice with the person?

- Discuss informally the learning your staff members are experiencing. Draw parallels with your experience so they might understand how to do your work should they decide to pursue your position or a similar one in the organization

Two Additional Actions:

1.

2.

Minstrelling: To minstrel is to reconcile the other eight educating types through storytelling and fostering the natural rhythms of learning and educating.

- Review what you know about yourself as you manage and lead through the eight other educating approaches.

- Encourage your staff to take up a path of learning, helpful to themselves, you, and others they work with.Explore how best to balance learning and action, helping your staff discover the dynamic balance between learning and action.

Two Additional Actions:

1.

2.

Return to the rafting story at the beginning of the Chapter, and identify where *facilitating, mentoring, and minstrelling* might apply.

Working Articles

Facilitating, mentoring, and minstrelling are critical yet misunderstood educating approaches within the workplace.

Often facilitating is a front for training or telling one's story. When you facilitate, you facilitate! When you train you train! When you lead you lead!

Mentoring can easily slide into telling one's story that sends a mentee down a rabbit hole. When you mentor, share wise practices that benefit the mentee.

Minstrelling involves competence in the eight other educating approaches singularly, and then, in combinations. Non-conscious, masterful competence in minstrelling evolves over time. Considerable reflection is required. Unfortunately, most manager-leaders fall short in their reflection in their use of the nine educating approaches as well as why and how they manage and lead.

Facilitation Insights Born of Experimentation and Experience

Here are 21 facilitating insights important to facilitators of meetings and staff learning processes.

1. Be Comfortable with Silence. Learn to walk a fine line between meeting the client's objectives and allowing the group to go where they need to go. If there is silence in the room, respect that. Don't try to fill it in with unwanted or unnecessary information. If the silence becomes uncomfortable for the group, or prolonged, you can provide a "process check" to determine the cause or perceived change of energy in the space and ask for individual feedback on this.

2. Be intuitive: Let your "gut reactions" or "sixth sense" be your guide. Be able to read what's not visible, as well as what's visible in the group. You may need to do "process checks" to validate these intuitive sensations. Be prepared to be flexible with where you are going and how to get there.

3. Be Participative: A good facilitator encourages the group to speak for itself. In recording words of the group, ensure you record THEIR words and not your interpretation of their words. Help them to clarify any confusion or disconnects they are communicating. Don't just act as an observer, be part of the introduction exercises, provide information about yourself that is engaging and relevant (your stories, your examples, analogies etc) to help reinforce your points. Engage with participants at breaks and lunches.

4. Clarify or Brief the reason for the facilitated session, and gain acceptance for participation as you may not get agreement for participation.

5. Call on your creativity: In the design of the session and "in the moment" don't be afraid to be creative and use new ways/exercises to provide an analogy or a simulation. Sometimes people do not "see" the learning only through text or a direct application – sometimes their learning is facilitated best through an indirect or seemingly unrelated activity. Here their defences get masked and their natural behaviour surfaces.

6. Complete a quick evaluation of the meeting. Ask what were the plus, minus and interesting aspects of the meeting. Take notes and improve at least one element of the meeting for next time.

7. Decide where to stand and sit in the room to facilitate the type of gathering you are attending. Can people enter and exit gracefully? Are you standing with your back to a window, etc?

8. Engage, engage, engage: As the group starts to enter the room, ensure that you welcome them to the session and ask some "safe" questions as a means

of introduction and initial engagement (weather, what division they work in or company they represent, how long have they been there, Any difficulties finding parking, etc.) Incorporating an ice-breaker or innovative way to initiate introductions starts the group off on the right foot. Providing some background as to why this session is happening is also useful – especially if someone has come to the wrong session. It's happened!

9. Ensure you have the necessary equipment to facilitate an event. Carry pens appropriate for flipchart paper, whiteboards, paper, masking tape, extra pens and pencils, sticky notes, paperclips or stapler, etc, with you. Never assume that what you need will be provided.

10. Facilitate so as not to facilitate: work yourself out of a job.

11. Focus on Application: Theory and rhetoric may be a quick way to impart information but it is not lasting. People need many structured opportunities throughout the session and subsequent to the workshop to apply the theory to real life situations, or simulations, and to learn from doing (praxis). It is through debriefing activities that many "ahas" occur for individuals.

12. Follow-through and Follow-up: One of the most important features of any good facilitation is the attention to follow-up and an evaluation of the impact of this session on future behaviour, attitudes, initiatives, etc. An opportunity to review learning, commitments, and shifts noted, or to provide a summary report on the session, must be built into every planned facilitation.

13. Frame the discussion points in an agenda: Use an agenda only as a template – be prepared to let the session be co-constructed "in the moment". However, make sure two topics are covered at minimum – What items are to inform? What items are to request insight?

14. Prepare, prepare, and prepare again: Prior to the session, research who is attending, the purpose of the session (stated and unstated), and any current issues between participants.   Organize appropriate materials/exercises based on this information. Also, ensure you know what to wear!

15. Record group memory on flipcharts that serves as visual reminders and/or complete 5 Minute Minutes using the headings Accountability, Collaborate, Responsibility, and Inform: Each decision assignment made during the meeting is categorized as Accountability (ability to account for), Collaborate (who to collaborate with), Responsibility (ability to respond to), and Inform (who to inform). The minutes are distributed immediately at the end of the meeting

16. Set up for Success: Ensure that the room set up is helpful for the type of session being held. Never scrimp on attention to detail such as ensuring the

availability of refreshments and lunch, as well as access to materials and AV aids. Allow for dialogue in smaller groups or dyads, as well as open space for large group discussion and set up so everyone has visual access to the AV equipment being used. I also like to vary the room set-up throughout a longer session (full day or longer) to encourage movement and more extensive dialogue.

17. Use collaborative learning techniques to increase participation and creative flow. Brain writing is an example; each person is given the same or a different question on a sheet of paper. They answer the question within a set time. Then the paper is rotated one position clockwise and the next person answers the question through adding to the first response and so on. Works best in groups of 3 to 5 people.

18. Wait through the silence when a question is asked. Wait until one of two things occur: either a person asks for clarification, or an attempt is made to answer your question

19. When needed, use your own life experiences to illustrate points. Your presence sets the mood and tone for the meeting.

20. When individuals challenge other people, encourage the challenge in the form of a question rather than as an 'attacking' statement.

21. Because silence was mentioned twice (#1 and #18), here are two additional ideas. First, silence is not consensus. Everyone's opinion matters; everyone needs to be heard! Second, silence is part of reflection. Some peoples' learning and personality preferences require time for reflection. In all ways, use silence to your advantage.

Thank you to Dr. Laurie Maslak for her contribution to this list and willingness to share her thoughts about facilitation.

Two Important Questions

Which insight calls to you and why?

Which insights are 'before you facilitate', 'as you facilitate' and 'after you facilitate'?

14 Important Truths for Mentor-Mentee Relationships

To mentor means to provide trusted advice to a mentee during her/his learning adventure. That is, mentors share the truth of their lived experiences when the mentees are ready (and sometimes not ready) to listen.

Mentors share their experiences in a friendly, conversational way. They have a vested interest in their mentees to gain personal insights into living their great lives and/or creating well-living workplaces.

> *My Mentors, My Mentoring*
>
> *I have had two notable mentors in my life. One was a playground supervisor when I was in my late teens. He showed me the path of creativity and freethinking. Through his encouragement I began to write poetry as a way to express my feelings. His spirit remains with me today even though I cannot remember his name.*
>
> *A second mentor gave me the gift of his time to dialogue so I might expand my ideas. Our conversations were glorious. When Gerard passed from this world, I bought a portion of his estate, re: the terms and concepts, processes and instruments to undertake organization culture assessment. Through continued research and considerable thinking, reflecting and presenting, I continue to honour our mentoring relationship by expanding our/my theory and practice.*
>
> *And today, I mentor others. I do so because 'you educate others about what you love to learn.' When I mentor, I pass along ideas, tools and techniques I have learned. More importantly, our conversations also generate new ideas that expand my thinking and practice.*

14 Truths about Mentoring

From a mentor-mentee perspective, here is what is important about mentoring:

1. The mentor starts from the perspective that the mentor is guiding the mentee to the mentee's knowing. They are both engaged in the social construction of knowledge, then wisdom.

2. The mentor connects with the identity the mentee offers. That is, the mentor starts with who the mentee is today. For example, if the person is opening a new business, the mentoring starts with entrepreneurship and the mentee being an entrepreneur. If the person is new to managing, the mentoring starts with management and the mentee being a manager. In doing so, there is shared context for the mentor's relationship with the mentee - a place to start that is accessible to both.

3.   Mentoring is a person-centred, learning-centred (humanistic) approach for shared trust, respect, fairness, caring, responsibility and a willingness to develop community.

4.   The mentor is most often asked to become engaged by the mentee. And yet, the mentor must have the wherewithal to know when the request would not benefit both parties and thus decline to become involved. The decision to mentor is with the mentor; this decision is sacred to the mentor.

5.   The mentor recognizes the mentee is on a learning journey (adventure) where and when the mentee may [or may not] request advice and guidance. Because of the trust and respect in the relationship, the mentor knows when to share and when to be quiet.

6.   The time spent together is usually of a duration that matches what the mentee's needs to learn from the mentor's lived experience.

7.   The shared (learning) conversation is dynamic, open and nurturing. Both intend to ensure what is said is relevant and applicable. Confidentiality is the glue that binds the relationship.

8.   The connection can be close in and/or far away. While face-to-face exchange has its advantages, technology-supported connections do allow for distance mentoring. However, there is something to be said for a real voice, seeing a real face and listening through body language.

9.   Mentors seek fair exchange in the relationship. While the mentor has a vested interest in the mentee gaining insight, the exchange has the mentor fulfilling a need to be in service. The view to serve originates from a sense of informed quietness.

10.   It is up to the mentee to use the insights gained from the conversation wisely. While the mentor helps lay out options, it is the mentee who makes the ethical decision to proceed.

11.   Mentors acknowledge and support mentees to continue their learning through the use of praise and the sharing of knowledge, skills and attitude insights.

12.   The mentoring and succession planning is more transformational than transactional. And yet, when possible, the relationship becomes transcendent. That is, individually and together, the mentor and mentee are going somewhere without either knowing where they will end up. Their relationship requires faith.

13. Each mentee is unique and deserves to be honoured and celebrated.

14. The mentor is a partner, a companion and a 'sage off the page.' The mentor counters feelings of loneliness along the mentee's journey. The mentee knows someone is present with whom to share thoughts and feelings.

These 14 insights are my truth about mentoring—a truth that continues to evolve; a truth, now articulated, that will see more light as it is shared with you.

Extending Your Learning

For your continued learning, here are questions to consider:

- Who has mentored you? What were the gifts of the mentoring?

- Who is mentoring you today?

- Who can you mentor?

- If approached to mentor someone, are you willing to say NO if there is no fit?

Minstrelling: About Integrating, Weaving, and Collaborating

When you minstrel, you use the additional processes of integrating, weaving, and collaborating.

To integrate means to combine into a vital whole, to demonstrate integrity in working with the given strategy

To weave means to interlace ideas to form a design, a structure

To collaborate means you base your relationships on assertiveness and cooperation.

As a minstrel, you obtain masterful competence in the other eight approaches. You see and feel your way through the use of the eight approaches integrating, weaving and collaborating with others effortlessly and to great acclaim.

Learners find themselves in a state of 'flow'; that is, time passes without distractions. Great learning occurs for them that has direct application afterwards. You educate through a dynamic balance of mixing and matching increasing challenge with competence improvement.

Four Minstrelling Tips

Through your concerted effort to use the *9 educating approaches,* you increase the self organizing ability of the learners. How you educate influences how they educate. It's a ripple effect!

Learners gain wider and deeper insight into their behavior and feelings through your use of the *9 educating approaches.* Know that how you educate has a great influence on learners' involvement moving forward.

Remember to get out of the way of learners when they know how to do it better than you; let them use the *9 educating approaches* in their interactions with others. Educate them in how to educate others, rather than simply educating them!

Seek out those who will help you educate, especially when you are not available. You help them grow in their competence. And, it frees you to continue your learning, for you educate what you love to learn.

Extending Your Learning

How might you know when you become a minstrel?

Whom do you know who uses a minstrel approach? How do you know it is a minstrel approach? What three aspects of their minstrelling approach might you use to help you further develop your educating approaches?

Chapter 7 Reflection

Having read Chapter 7, what are three insights you would draw from your learning? And why are they important to you today?

Insight 1 and its importance >

Insight 2 and its importance >

Insight 3 and its importance >

For further tips, tools, and techniques about the 9 educating approaches visit:

www.managingleading.com/cpages/9educating-approaches

Chapter 8:
Educator Within = integration
of the 9 approaches

Competency: Are you competent to ___ Yes or No:

1. Discuss how the educating approaches working as a whole support managing and leading in the workplace.

2. Review and discuss five examples that involve one or more educating approaches as a way to summarize learning.

3. Discuss the concept of 'courage' to act.

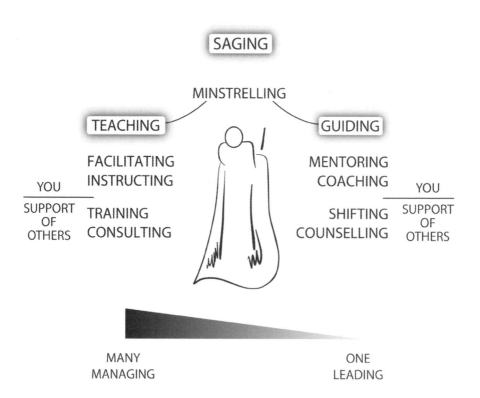

Exploring the commitment to the 9 approaches as a whole

Please read the story that follows.

Whitewater Rafting Story Continues

Sharing time at the end of the trip, Jan, Jonathan and Herbert thanked Hobbit for his generosity throughout the trip. The three kids, in their own unique ways, thanked Hobbit, as well.

"It was great having you along on the trip. And it is wonderful you got a little extra out of the trip," Hobbit said as he stood by Jonathan's vehicle. "You did great today with the raft. And I hope your nervousness is gone about playing with water."

Jonathan was nodding, "More than you know. You were great. And I know the kids really appreciated your time with them as well. You are a great educator!"

"I will take that as a compliment. Thanks! Well, you'd best get going as you have a long drive home. Enjoy the journey." As the jeep pulled away, Hobbit waved.

Turning around, Hobbit saw Jan, Herbert and the kids heading towards him in their vehicle. Rolling down his window, Herbert reached out his hand and shook Hobbit's hand. "It was great. Thanks ever so much. You got me thinking about using what you talked about back in the workplace. Here is my card.   Send me an email, and we will get together. Again, thanks!"

"Safe journey home!" With that, Hobbit smiled and stepped away from the car as the family pulled away. He waved goodbye.

Worksheet for Integrating the 9 Educating Approaches

Deciding on an Educating Approach to Complement the Situation

Whether managing and/or leading others, it is important to select an educating approach that works best for the situation. Consider the five examples listed below and identify the 3 educating approach(es) you would most likely use for that situation.

Instructing: To instruct is to provide a description and explanation of the knowledge and/or skill at a deeper level.

Training: To train is to impart some particular skill with some knowledge for immediate use.

Consulting: To consult is to provide information and/or to exchange ideas.

Coaching: To coach is to drive and/or urge participation through the task.

Shifting: To shift is to support understanding of personal career decisions.

Counselling: To counsel is to talk things over and to listen with caring.

Facilitating: To facilitate is to help a process go well, to draw out from the person/people blue-sky ideas.

Mentoring: To mentor is to provide trusted advice during the adventure.

Minstrelling: To minstrel is to reconcile the other eight educating types through storytelling and fostering the natural rhythms of learning and educating.

1) Call centre staff have been given a new software program to use.

1st _____   2nd _____   3rd _____

Why?

2) Twenty-one high calibre candidates identified through performance reviews are asked to learn about leadership to shape and guide the organization over the next 10 years.

1st _____   2nd _____   3rd _____

Why?

3) Three managers, each with 10 years of experience, have transferred to a different country to take up their job assignments in order to expand business operations.

1st _____   2nd _____   3rd _____

Why?

4) Four front-line health-care employees have been coming to work late, and as their supervisor you decide to work with them on a time management program.

1st _____   2nd _____   3rd _____

Why?

5) The senior executive has invited you to the organization's annual meeting to share your department's story about the new educating initiative you started. Explain how it works and why it is important for others to use the *9 educating approaches*.

1st _____   2nd _____   3rd _____

Why?

Having learned about the 9
educating approaches, the time has come to
move your learning into action.

In moving into action,
make a commitment to use
the 9 educating approaches in how
you manage-lead, starting today.

You and your staff will appreciate your
efforts. Even with mistakes, there is more
learning. When you help your staff to help
you manage and lead, the successes and
mistakes they experience with you add to
their learning and your educating.

In order to bridge the 9 educating
approaches with your action of
managing and leading, the following
pages in this chapter highlight making
and fulfilling commitment.

What sets you apart from others is the character and courage of your commitments ….

What is a Commitment?

A commitment is a promise to do something. To make a commitment is to bind you intellectually and emotionally to a course of action.

Underpinning the concept of *commitment* is the concept of *decisions*. You decide on your commitments from a series of choices. Then, you decide whether or not to meet these commitments.

Keeping commitments builds trust; not keeping commitments breaks trust. Though many people distinguish between commitments that "count" and those that don't, it's guaranteed that if you don't keep commitments in one area of your life, it shows up in other areas as well.

Whether in your personal life or in business, the commitments you make and keep define you. Personal examples include showing up on time, being present, and "being there" for the friends and family to whom you've promised to listen to. Business examples include delivering on time and not over-promising, maintaining the agreed upon standard of quality, and meeting payment terms.

Commitments and Estimates

Commitments are different from estimates.

In listening to what people will deliver, most statements are framed as estimates. "I will have something on your desk in about a week," is an estimate, whereas "I will write a preliminary report and have it on your desk by Friday noon," is a commitment.

An estimate is not a commitment, and the difference between the two is significant.

> The essence of an estimate is *expectation*. When you give an estimate, you express your expectations about what will happen. Hesitation is built into each estimate.

The essence of a commitment is *promise*. A commitment is a pledge. When you make a commitment, you declare your intention to create something, and you invite yourself to fulfill your intention.

If you treat estimates as commitments, there is a high probability you will be disappointed. Think back over the last couple of weeks, and re-listen to what was said to you, especially where you felt disappointment afterwards.

What was said about what? Take a few minutes and reflect on some conversations.

The Courage for Your Commitments

With commitments, you must find the courage to fulfill your promise.

If an adjustment is required in fulfilling your promise, then you express the alteration to those you have promised, and make a recommitment.

Courage is a character skill. Courage is about finding the strength of mind to deal with your fear when you encounter difficult situations.

Within your very being, you find the ways and means to ensure your commitments are upheld. And yet, in being human, you forgive yourself when a commitment requires alteration.

The spirit that surrounds your commitment is the desire to keep the commitment, and not get into a habit of breaking them.

Questions about Your Managing-Leading Commitments

What management or leadership commitments did you make last week? Did you fulfil them? If not, what did you do about dealing with your shortfall?

What management or leadership commitments do you have this week? Will you fulfil them or do you need to alter your intention and recommitment?

What actions will you take when your PEERS do not fulfil their commitments?

What actions will you take when your MANAGERS' commitments are not fulfilled?

What actions will you take when your CLIENTS' commitments are not fulfilled?

What actions will you take when OTHERS' commitments are not fulfilled?

What actions will you take when YOUR commitments are not fulfilled?

Have you celebrated your courage in fulfilling your management and leadership commitments? If not, I encourage you do so!

Seven major commitments helpful in using educating as a way of managing and leading others

You will commit to:

1] <u>Living Your Great Life</u> which means honouring reality while living from your vision, which entails not trying to fake it. Being committed to reality means responding to life's challenges and generating opportunities for celebrations.

2] <u>Fair Exchange</u> which means developing your capacity to be psychologically self-sufficient while engaging the hands, heads, and hearts of others.

3] <u>Ethics and Educating</u> which means deciding to educate through a set of ethical values that serve everyone involved directly and indirectly.

4] <u>Purpose</u> which means being vision and goal-oriented, which entails not drifting aimlessly from one episode of your life to the next, from one work commitment to another.

5] <u>Contribution</u> which means creating value in some situation. Being committed to usefulness means responding to life's challenges by not throwing your arms up in despair, but rather by actively seeking opportunities to create value for self and with others.

6] <u>Listening and Learning</u> which means applying thought to the circumstances of your living your great life, which entails making sure your thoughts and ideas correspond to reality and you share in ways that are understandable to others.

7] <u>Individual Rights</u> which means defending your own rights and spurning opportunities to gain advantages at the cost of violating the rights of others.

10 Considerations for Making and Keeping Commitments

Commitments are an essential element of using education as a way of managing and leading. Making commitments is how you move things forward and grow relationships.

Here are 10 considerations for making and keeping commitments:

1. Resist the urge to immediately make a commitment if you're unsure you can keep it.

2. Make a commitment with conditions that address the unknown, or specify a later parameter for making a firm commitment.

3. Affirm with the other person that the conditions are understood.

4. Check in and communicate often about the commitments you've made. If something looks like it will slip, let the other person know about it sooner rather than later.

5. Use an action management system to know what commitments are scheduled and what advance actions are necessary to fulfill them.

6. Admit when you break a commitment and take steps to deal with the potential damage.

7. Communicate with the other person if the commitment will not be fulfilled as agreed upon. Ask them how it can be made correct, and be willing to take those steps. Sincerely apologize.

8. Take care not to let breaking commitments become a pattern, or your commitments will not be taken seriously in the future.

9. Frame your commitment to your behaviour and not an outcome.

10. Make commitments in great faith and with great intention.

Your Additional Notes:

Chapter 8 Reflection

Having read Chapter 8, what are three insights you would draw from your learning? And why are they important to you today?

Insight 1 and its importance >

Insight 2 and its importance >

Insight 3 and its importance >

Chapter 9:
Discover Educating as a Way to Manage and Lead

Competency: Are you competent to ___ Yes or No:

1. Discuss briefly the connection between managing and leading.

2. Review and discuss the linkages between managing/leading and educating approaches.

3. Value which educating approaches are to be mastered for leading and those where you ask others to help you lead.

4. Value which educating approaches are to be mastered for managing and those where you ask others to help you manage.

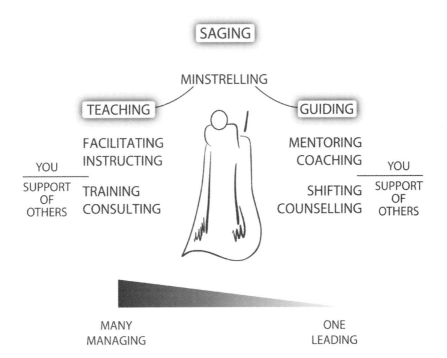

This chapter explores the relationship among managing and leading and the *9 educating approaches* as a whole.

Please read the story that follows.

Whitewater Raft: A Metaphor

A couple of hours before the rafting trip starts, the guides and trip leader get together to go over the operations for the day. This daily connection ensures everyone is ready for the trip, especially if the weather conditions have altered the characteristics of the river flow.

On some rivers that are dam fed, the water level is usually the same for the day. On free flow rivers, the warming sun can bring more water out of the mountains in the afternoon and/or if there has been rainfall the day before it may show up as a surge the next day. Also, if rain is anticipated there may be thunder and lightning—with hail possible—within sight of the mountains.

Therefore, change is present every day. It includes all 'outside in' factors that influence the experience, like weather and river flow. With this awareness, the crew has to adjust to meet the conditions. They must dynamically balance the 'outside in' factors with 'inside out' factors like proper equipment preparation, on-water trip commands, and proper alignment through rapids.

The preparation of the clients is important through safety talks, demonstrating paddling techniques and explaining what to do if a client has an 'out-of-boat experience'. Therefore, all of the guides and trip leaders use basic educating approaches to lead and manage a great trip experience for the clients assigned to them.

Connecting You as Manager/Leader with the 9 Educating Approaches

No matter what situation you find yourself in as a manager/leader ...

What is good now, can be great now;

What is 'ho-hum' now can be great sooner than you know.

In using the *9 educating approaches*, you *Help Them to Help YOU Manage and Lead*. That is, you manage and lead others to create a place of work where and when everyone works well together. A work place where everyone likes what they do and does what they like.

What becomes important to everyone involved is for you to manage and lead to the best of your capabilities. Therefore, it is important you become competent in the educating approaches found in this Book.

Before connecting the 9 *educating approaches* with managing and leading, it is helpful to reconnect with the managing and leading table offered in Chapter 2. You completed the table earlier.

Management, Managing, Manager	Leadership, Leading, Leader
Tell Others	Ask a Person
Dance Floor, Sitting Down, In	Balcony, Standing Up, On
Responsibility	Accountability
Evaluating with Others	Reflecting with Self
Innovation	Creativity
Debriefing	Briefing
Discussion and Debate	Dialogue
Motivation	Inspiration
Reward	Recognition
Tactical Plan	Strategic Map

When leading, master coaching and mentoring and ask for help with shifting and counselling

Who do you ask for help with shifting and counselling in your organization?

Where can you learn about coaching and mentoring?

~~~~~~~~~~   ~~~~~~~~~~

When managing, master facilitating and instructing and ask for help with training and consulting

Who do you ask for help with training and consulting in your organization and outside your organization?

Where can you learn about facilitating and instructing?

Chapter 9 Reflection

Having read Chapter 9, what are three insights you would draw from your learning? And why are they important to you today?

Insight 1 and its importance >

Insight 2 and its importance >

Insight 3 and its importance >

Chapter 10:
Awaken the Educator Within, Leverage the Educating Without

Competency: Are you competent to ____ Yes or No:

1. Outline the state of the workplace.

2. Define the term and concepts: **awaken, educator within, leverage, and educating without.**

3. Link educating approaches to staff engagement, retention and performance improvement.

4. Link educating approaches to personal succession mapping.

State of the Workplace

The following selection of statistics is an indicator of the state of the workplace from engagement, retention, and performance perspectives. They are taken from various surveys conducted from 2009 through 2011.

Worker Satisfaction
- Out of 10,914 workers surveyed by Blessing White, only 31 per cent are engaged.
- Fewer than 1 in 3 employees worldwide (31%) are engaged. Nearly 1 in 5 (17%) are actively disengaged.
- Trust in executives can have more than twice the impact on engagement levels than trust in immediate managers does.
- Employees worldwide who know their managers as "people," are more likely to be engaged.
- The higher up in the organization you go, the more likely you are to be engaged.
- Engagement levels are higher among older employees and people in positions of power and authority.
- Engagement increases with organizational tenure.

Source: *2011 Employee Engagement Report, Blessing White*
http://www.blessingwhite.com/eee__report.asp

88% - The percentage of **fully engaged** employees who believe they can positively impact the quality of their organization's products and services.

38% - The percentage of **disengaged** employees who feel the same way.

Source: Employee Engagement Surveys, Towers Watson
http://www.towerswatson.com/services/Employee-Surveys

- Companies in the top 10 per cent on employee engagement bested their competition by 72 per cent in earnings per share during 2007-08. For companies that scored beneath the top quartile, earnings fell 9.4 per cent below their competition.
- Gallup researchers, who base the Employee Engagement Index on a survey of nearly 42,000 randomly selected adults, estimate that disengaged workers cost U.S. businesses as much as $350 billion a year.
- 33 per cent of workers are engaged in their jobs, 49 per cent are not engaged, and 18 per cent are actively disengaged. The Gallup Organization defines the categories as follows:
  - Engaged employees work with passion and feel a profound connection to their company. They drive innovation and move the organization forward.
  - Non-engaged employees have essentially "checked out." They sleepwalk through workdays. They put in time but don't approach their work with energy or passion.
  - Actively disengaged employees aren't just unhappy at work; they're busy acting out their unhappiness. Every day, these workers undermine what engaged co-workers accomplish.

Source: Raising Engagement, SHRM
http://www.shrm.org/Publications/hrmagazine/
EditorialContent/2010/0510/Pages/0510fox.aspx

As new State of Workplace
studies and their statistics
become available, please visit
www.managingleading.com/cpages/9Educating-Approaches
for updates.

Worksheet – Situational Use of *9 Educating Approaches*

Having read the statistics above, how might each of the *9 educating approaches* be helpful in dealing with the situations presented?

Instructing

Training

Consulting

Coaching

Shifting

Counselling

Facilitating

Mentoring

Minstrelling

The above mentioned statistics were pulled from various studies because they highlight four important aspects of the manager-leaders' work with others.

They are (and not in priority as that decision is yours to make):

Engagement: The statistics highlight a high level of non-engagement of staff. That is, staff are not working to their full potential for reasons identified above. Yet, your organization has its own challenges. Do you know the top three?

1.

2.

3.

It's common that staff often leave the manager-leader more times than they leave the organization. Therefore, retention is an issue you have to address by awakening to who you are in relationship to your staff based on the engagement challenges you face.

Retention: The statistics highlight people who are looking to move to another workplace.

This looking elsewhere takes energy away from their work. In other words, your staff is distracted. Their performance by outcome diminishes over time.

Performance Improvement: The statistics highlight the observation that when effort is given to support performance improvement, there is increased worker satisfaction with maximization of productivity.

Equally important is your need to remain in continuous learning to become competent and retain continuance in why and how you manage and lead.

Manager-Leader Progression: For you to succeed and continue on your career path, you must find ways to balance the positive and negative issues highlighted by the statistics when it comes to managing and leading engagement, retention and performance improvement.

Therefore, one of the best ways to help your staff help you manage-lead is to use the *9 Educating Approaches* highlighted in this book.

Throughout this book, the case is made for you to value the *9 educating approaches* as an insightful and practical technique to leverage ways to engage and retain your staff.

Awakening the educator within to leverage the educating without involves important competencies you need to integrate into your portfolio. See the competency list highlighted earlier in the book. Revisit your earlier self-assessment and determine next steps in weaving the *9 educating approaches* into how you manage and lead.

Awaken the Educator Within

> **Awaken:** To become aware of something; to bring into perspective.

> **Educator within:** To become aware of the educator within you because when you share, you educate. Therefore, in every way during every day when you share, you educate.

Leverage the Educating Without

> **Leverage:** To use something to your advantage; to use the power to act effectively.

> **Educating Without:** To leverage your managing-leading through use of the *9 educating approaches* to encourage engagement, maintain retention, and improve performance of your staff   while you enhance your personal succession as a manager-leader

Career Note: If you are a Manager-Leader

Developing your management-leadership talent is a long-term investment. When adding to your portfolio of why and how to manage and lead, use the *9 Educating Approaches* to position yourself as someone interested in staff engagement, retention and performance improvement. More so, you will stand out among other applicants as someone who has the solution!

Therefore, in choosing between two or more qualified people for a new management-leadership position, when the hiring group considers YOU they will clearly see that you have the "know-why" and know-how of the *9 Educating Approaches*.

AND because of your application of the *9 Educating Approaches,* you have:
- prepped others to take your position;
- prepared others to be ready and able to step up when needed.

Worksheet – Thoughts and Feelings

Awaken the Educator Within

What thoughts and feelings hinder or hold you back in awakening the educator within?

What thoughts and feelings help or move you forward in awakening the educator within?

Leverage the Educating Without

What thoughts and feelings hinder or hold you back from leveraging the educating without?

What thoughts and feelings help or move you forward in leveraging the educating without?

Worksheet – What needs to be true?

The most important question at this point in the book:

For you to be an awesome workplace educator – recognized by your staff and colleagues in using the 9 Educating Approaches as you manage and lead – what needs to be true in your organization?

The comments written into Chapter 10 are insights
helpful in editing/writing your work plans
and personal development plan.

Chapter 11 helps you focus your learning to action
for a particular workplace challenge. In addition,
you are prompted to complete a personal
"Action Map" to apply learning from
this book immediately!

Chapter 10 Reflection

Having read Chapter 10, what are three insights you would draw from your learning? And why are they important to you today?

Insight 1 and its importance >

Insight 2 and its importance >

Insight 3 and its importance >

Chapter 11:
Taking It to Work: Action Mapping

Competency: Are you competent to ___ Yes or No:

1. Apply 9+1 suggestions for educating others when starting with self.

2. Review an Action Mapping process to guide your transfer of learning.

> **Educating demonstrates that things are possible.**
> **Learning is making it possible for you.**
> **Anonymous**

This chapter encourages you to act; that is, to manage, lead and educate. It encourages you to educate what you desire to learn through your commitments to action and continuous learning.

Consider

It is one thing to be educated in something. It is yet another thing to do something with what you learned. This book makes it possible to learn about the linkages among the 9 *educating approaches* and managing-leading.

Now, you are encouraged to use the learning you take from this book. And in turn, you are requested to contribute to the body of knowledge and skill that others will draw from in helping themselves and others in living their great lives, creating the well-living workplace, and co-creating the well-living world.

In an effort to move your learning to knowing, the 9+1 insights for educating others, when starting with yourself, are found below. The insights list what is important to know in **stepping up** in your use of 9 *educating approaches* as a way to manage and lead.

Also, the Action Mapping process that follows the Summary List has you identify a work-related challenge that can be served by your use of one or more of the *9 educating approaches* discovered through this book.

Print this page:

9+1 Suggestions for Educating Others When Starting with Self

1. Know thyself. Continue to learn about who you are for yourself to be with others.

2. Demonstrate listening. Look up, turn to face the person, and engage both ears.

3. Determine your voice. Share your authenticity while being conscious of your position and authority.

4. Know your body language. Voice follows gesture; when necessary, exaggerate.

5. Inspire from the balcony. Motivate from the dance floor.

6. Find the lighter side of work. Shine your light there and lessen the burden while encouraging fun with and among others.

7. Commit to act. Keep your promises; help others to help you manage and lead

8. Review helpful educating approaches. Hone your skills, gather new knowledge, and share with others.

9. Connect with accelerated learning-for-knowing. Celebrate the product, encourage the process, and share abundantly.

+1. When you listen, you learn. When you share, you educate. ...

Action MAP for Your Workplace Issue

*Managing/Leading through a Perspective Map of a Work-Related Challenge
to which Educating Approaches can be Applied*

The Purpose of this Mapping Activity

This activity will assist you in developing a viable Action Map related to a "real life" staff challenge. Your involvement in this activity will help you to consolidate the knowledge and ideas you have gained through this book. In addition, it will enable you to apply the educating concepts, tools, and approaches discussed in the book in a meaningful and action-oriented manner.

The Process

Challenge Identification

The first step is to identify a "real-life" work-related challenge you are confronted with in your current position: one that requires you to manage and/or lead.

>> In selecting your challenge, choose something within your ability
to control or at least significantly influence/coordinate.

>> The challenge does not have to be a problem – a situation where you have a concern. Instead, you may have a situation where something is working well and you wish to expand it. You appreciate something that is useful and see benefit in helping others learn about it.

Your Challenge

Write a short statement that describes your challenge in such a way that someone who is unfamiliar with your situation would be able to understand it.

Description:

With this challenge in mind, answer the Perspective Questions that follow:

What vision are you working from? What do you specifically want to achieve as you understand the challenge from a satellite or bird's eye perspective?

Why is your challenge important? What are the consequences if it is not addressed? What are the benefits if it is addressed?

How urgent is your challenge? Why? What are the implications if you do nothing?

How will you proceed? Consider innovative/creative solutions you have not used before.

What physical, capital, and infrastructure resources will you require?

Who should be involved? Who can help? Who might hinder? For those who might hinder, how will you persuade them to assist you?

What, if any, obstacles do you anticipate? How will you overcome these?

When do you expect it to be started and completed? Identify some milestones.

Select three "what if" scenarios:

*Example: **What if** they come wanting more than I can offer? I will engage a few to educate the rest.*

What if ____? I will–

What if ____? I will–

What if ____? I will-

Other thoughts ...

Linking Managing and Leading with Educating

Your Challenge

For the challenge you described above, is it necessary for you to manage and/or lead the situation? Circle the best response.

Lead   **Manage**   **Both**

Of the *9 educating approaches* listed below, which two approaches would serve you best in managing and/or leading the situation described above?

Instructing: To instruct is to provide a description and explanation of the knowledge and/or skill at a deeper level.

Training: To train is to impart some particular skill with some knowledge for immediate use.

Consulting: To consult is to provide information and/or to exchange ideas.

Coaching: To coach is to drive and/or urge participation through the task.

Shifting: To shift is to support understanding of personal career decisions.

Counselling: To counsel is to talk things over and to listen with caring.

Facilitating: To facilitate is to help a process go well, to draw out from the person/people blue-sky ideas.

Mentoring: To mentor is to provide trusted advice during the adventure.

Minstrelling: To minstrel is to reconcile the other eight educating types through storytelling and fostering the natural rhythms of learning and educating.

First choice and why?

Second choice and why?

**From your responses on the previous page, write down
three 'actions' you will take to influence the outcome
of the challenge you identified starting tomorrow.**

1:

2:

3:

Your versatility in applying what you learn from this book will help you be the best for those you serve, as you manage and lead while educating.

Last Reflection

Before closing the book with summary thoughts, there is one last task for you to complete. It's possibly the most important!

The task involves you pinpointing three actions you will take to purposefully apply the learning achieved from reading this book and completing the worksheets, and put those actions into practice.

It is important you practice what you've learned. The Action Mapping tool on the next page has been proven to be an excellent way to summarize what you learn and to identify how to take learning and move it to practice.

An example of how to use the Action Mapping tool is provided.

Action Mapping Chart

Your name: _____ Date:_____

"I have the ultimate accountability to acquire the knowledge, skills, and experience needed to meet the challenge identified above and/or other challenges I will encounter. Therefore, I commit to the following actions."

Fill in the chart using the Continue, Start, and Stop action verbs listed in the table. By signing this map, you promise to achieve these commitments by the date identified in the right hand column.

Example:

	What is one thing you will do?	Detail when, where and with what resources	Who is involved and why?	How will you know it is done?
Example	Share insights from additional books read on using educating as a way to manage and lead	Seek book summary companies; work with the interlibrary system at work; chat with other managers about what they are reading; complete a Google search; use the resource list provided in this book	Library staff; other managers in the know; my mentor and coach; those who have insights	Develop a resource page that I send to others; present summary of learning to other managers each month

	What is one thing you will do?	Detail when, where and with what resources	Who is involved and why?	How will you know it is done?
1	CONTINUE to do (something that is working)			
2	START to do (something you believe will help)			
3	STOP doing (something that is working)			

Use another page if needed.

Signed: _____ Date: _____

Chapter 11 Reflection

Having read Chapter 11, what are three insights you would draw from your learning? And why are they important to you today?

Insight 1 and its importance:

Insight 2 and its importance:

Insight 3 and its importance:

Chapter 12:
Closing Thoughts

Help Them Help YOU Manage-Lead

Use the 9 *educating approaches*
as a way to manage-lead,

to encourage engagement,

to support retention,

to improve performance,

to assist personal progression,

to awaken the Educator Within,
and to leverage the Educating Without.

And when you manage and lead, think about how
to support yourself and others to work **SMARTER**.

As you help them to help you manage and lead, make sure you help them:

Be **S**pecific in their work
Do what **M**atters every day
Achieve their objectives
Be **R**ealistic in what they complete
Do work in a **T**imely fashion
Energetically finish every project
Be **R**ecognized for a job well done

Ask yourself how you can be SMARTER, as well.

Be mindful, heartfelt as you:

Think strategically

Decide expeditiously

Execute decisively

Communicate effectively

Manage honourably

Lead extensively

Share authenticity

Ready hospitality

Encourage Involvement

Celebrate Your Achievements
Celebrate Their Accomplishments

For further tips, tools, and techniques
on the 9 educating approaches visit:

www.managingleading.com/cpages/9educating-approaches

Appendices

Chapter 1: Suggested Responses to Questions by Chapter

Chapter 2: Connecting Educating with Managing and Leading

**Mix and Match Key Connectors
Between Management and Leadership**

Management, Managing, Manager	Leadership, Leading, Leader
Tell Others	Ask Others
Dance Floor	Balcony
Responsibility	Accountability
Evaluating with Others	Reflecting with Self
Innovation	Creativity
Debriefing	Briefing
Discussion and Debate	Dialogue
Motivation	Inspiration
Reward	Recognition
Tactical Plan	Strategic Map

Chapter 5: Training, Consulting, Instructing:

10 new recruits were hired on Tuesday to support the 'call-out program' informing past clients of the new products and services offered by the company after the recent merger. New phone systems with hands-free features were installed on Monday.

Instructing	**Training**	Consulting

Three recently promoted group managers approached you with an employee engagement issue from their work area.

Instructing	Training	**Consulting**

Two emergent leaders from another part of the organization asked you to lunch to discuss the roll-out of the new principle-centred negotiation program you developed for project management in international settings. They have had limited success in implementing the program in their African operations. They are in for two days attending meetings and emailed you to set up the four hour meeting.

Instructing	Training	Consulting

Chapter 6: Coaching, Shifting, Counselling:

Friday, mid-afternoon, you notice Mary-Jane slumped over her desk. She looks exhausted. When you ask her what is happening, she says her two college aged children are coming in for the weekend and she is not ready. She hasn't done the shopping or cleaned the house. She has been working overtime all week. As Mary-Jane's manager, you wonder how you can help her.

Coaching   Shifting   **Counselling**

A long-term client has complained about the service he has received over the past six months. He is willing to give you another chance before pulling the account. He enjoys working with you because you hold him accountable for his actions. However, he has voiced displeasure with the paperwork he has to complete. Also, he mentioned he seems to get lost in the shuffle. He is not computer savvy and freely admits that point.

Coaching   Shifting   Counselling

For many weeks now, Eileen has been sharing her love for web design. During the past year, she has been studying in the evenings at a community college. On recent numerous occasions, she has voiced her displeasure about her job. As the mid-level manager of the consulting company for which she works, you heard her tell her story again at lunch.

Coaching   **Shifting**   Counselling

Chapter 7: Facilitating, Mentoring, Minstrelling:

Jonathan is a senior engineer who is well-liked by his colleagues. In about two months, he will be transferring to the Hawaiian office where he will retire in another three years. He has a wealth of knowledge and skill that he is willing to share with a few colleagues. He has said he is willing to 'hold court,' a term he affectionately uses to describe the time spent sharing his thoughts with the younger engineers.

Facilitating   Mentoring   **Minstrelling**

Joshua, a Gen-Xer, is a recent Master's graduate in leadership who has been working in your unit for the past six months. He is a little brash at times, and he has made it known he wants to move on. During your bi-weekly coffee with him yesterday, he mentioned an opening was available in the parent company office. He is seeking some advice.

Facilitating   **Mentoring**   Minstrelling

You have been hired to reorganize a department in a Caribbean resort. For the past two years, the department has received low ratings from its staff and the clients have been commenting on declining service quality. Some clients have gone so far as to say they will not be returning. Next Tuesday is your first day.

Facilitating   Mentoring   Minstrelling

Bonus:

**Having read this far in the book, if you email
info@managingleading.com
with either a positive, one-word description or submit a
50-100 word short testimonial about the book**
(with your name, city, country)
[work title and workplace name is optional]

**you'll receive a free copy of the eBook
*Creating the Well-Living Workplace***
(retails at C$21.95).

In addition, tap into the ongoing conversation about managing and
leading and the 9 educating approaches through
www.managingleading.com/cpages/9educating-approaches

Chapter 9: Connecting with 9 Educating Approaches

The answers below are my suggestions to further your learning.

However, having read the book, you may see a different combination of approaches.

1) Call centre staff have been given a new software program to use.

   1st _Training   2nd _Coaching

2) Twenty-one high calibre candidates identified through performance reviews are asked to learn about leadership to shape and guide the organization over the next 10 years.

   1st _Instructing   2nd _Mentoring   3rd _Shifting

3) Three managers, each with 10 years of experience, have transferred to a different country
to take up their job assignments in order to expand business operations.

   1st _Facilitating   2nd _Consulting   3rd _Shifting

4) Four front-line health-care employees have been coming to work late and as their supervisor you decide to work with them on a time management program.

   1st _Counselling   2nd _Coaching_

5) The senior executive has invited you to the organization's annual meeting to share your department's story about the new educating initiative you started, explain how it works, and why it is important for others to use the *9 educating approaches*.

   1st _Minstrelling   2nd _Instructing

Introducing the Author

Stephen Hobbs, Ed.D., founded and serves as Master Navigator and Educator with WELLth Learning Network. With the assistance of dedicated WELLth Educators, Stephen helps ecologically inspired entrepreneurs to dynamically balance their wellth creation and wealth creation decisions. In addition, he guides entrepreneurs with staff to create workplaces where everyone enjoys what they do and do what they enjoy.

Steve's interests and contributions include navigating organizational culture, management excellence, leadership magnificence, workforce learning, workplace educating, experience-based learning, and visual mapping.

He has written and self-published books such as **Creating the Well-Living Workplace** (WELLTH, 2010), **Living YOUR Great Life** (WELLTH, 2010), and **Co-Creating the WELL-Living World** (2010).

Help Them Help You Manage-Lead is his fifth book.

Two additional books will be available in 2013 called **The Ultimate Guide to Listening for Managing and Leading** and **Simple and Practical Ethical Decision Making Guide for Everyone in the Workplace**

He balances his life with mentoring, writing, walking, and cooking gluten-free/lactose-free meals. World travel is his love as evident in his 20 year odyssey to live and work around the world (he started August 2011). More insights and his travels are available through www.IAmMyOffice.com

Contact Coordinates:
ManagingLeading.com
info@ManagingLeading.com

WELLthLearning.com
info@WELLthLearning.com

1.403.875.0449

Index